The Rebel Radio Diary

LPR La Prensa Rebelde

The Rebel Radio Diary

A social-historical political-intrigue, poetic travelogue set in Cuba

Rupert Mould

LPR - NINJA TUNE

Edited by Alice Grandison - freelance editor/Canongate Books, Edinburgh

Published by 'la prensa rebelde – LPR'
'LPR' logo by Ral Veroni
Front cover photograph by Emmanuel Georges – glass-plate photographer of Cuban classic automobiles.
For further information contact: e.georges@evc.net

First issued with 'The Cuban Master Sessions Series,
Calle 23, Havana'
Commercially released by 'Ninja Tune Records', London, England
Albums released in two parts throughout the years 2000 - 2001

ISBN 0-9538553-0-9

Cover design, layout and typesetting by Haydn Suckling
email: haydn@nildram.co.uk

Visit the 'Up, Bustle and Out' website for film footage, information on 'LPR' publications, press reviews, causes and actions, discography, DJ gig guide, poetry and a literary criticism collection, music and fantasy - all at:
http://www.upbustleandout.pwp.blueyonder.co.uk

'The smokeyness of Bristol, the coolness of Havana
Peaceful in the desert, Rebels in the crowd'

Contact us at: e-mail rebel.radio@blueyonder.co.uk

Many thanks to:

Dr Roderick Watson - English Department, University of Stirling, Scotland, Alice Grandison for her time and attention on this manuscript, Ral Veroni, Ninja Tune Records - London and Montreal, Radio Rebelde - La Habana, Cuba, Emmanuel Georges, Jules 'Shoes' Elvins, Miles Essex, Javier Cerdas, 'Clandestine Ein' – the beat impostor, Graham Greene – where loyalties feint – en paz señor, Orquesta Richard Egües and Invitados, Estudio Sonocaribe - La Habana, Cuba, Sally and Susan Mould, Bab, my late Grandfather for the spirit of adventure passed on to me, 'Tío Cocinando' and Mijail Arteaga... each and every one who has supported 'Up, Bustle and Out' over the years – gracias queridos amigos, sigamos luchando...

Sᵢʀ:

Since I know that you will be pleased at the great victory with which Our Lord has crowned my voyage. I write this to you, from which you will learn how in thirty-three days I reached the Indies, with the fleet which the most illustrious King and Queen, our Sovereigns, gave to me. There I found very many islands, filled with people without number, and I have taken possession of them all for Their Highnesses, by proclamation and with the royal standard unfurled, and no objection was offered to me.

(Columbus' Letter To Ferdinand and Isabella, 1493)

Lines of poetry rear like waves; they shatter noisily or move heavily like wild beasts in a cage, and in untameable and tragic disorder like seas slapping against a ship's hull. It seems as if a sombre spirit, clothed in black and swiftly ascending through lugubrious space, were hiding its wounds and escaping from the poetry. How strange that those dark garments should fly open and release a bouquet of roses!

Flowers of exile!

(José Martí, quotation from an introduction to 'Flowers Of Exile')

Public applause

A hero of historic revolution speaks:

'The Matador's eyes focused coldly in his artful pose—
where whispered the silver of the sword's blade
towards the looming, fractured presence of Africa—
who came speechless to our shores.

'Exposed rows of whitish teeth – froze.
The moment to prey had arrived.
Black confronted Black – Matador and Bull – eye to eye
Twisting – one with the sweat of glory – molten
argent running in a bead down his temple – the other
sunk shamefully upon his knees where flowed a river—
                a River of Blood.

'Between the Mediterranean landscapes,
tragically separated billions of years ago,
the blue sea comforts crimson alluvia, glinting
along the echoes that cried and died in a silver—
splintering, sparking public applause:

                'Olé!' they shouted – '¡Muerte!'

'They threw the symbolic roses in:
deep red roses that drifted out to sea
along this River of Blood.

'I witnessed the looming shadow
of a continent retreat—then repeat,
there stepped into the arena a Child –
        a Wild impoverished Child.
She wore only one black shoe and a label:

        Sent by Russia to beg for bread

        'S i l e n c e –

"She stirred daintily until judgement was passed,

        'Gracias, good and gracious God for Russia,
        She's our New Africa – ¡Olé!

        'New Africa, New Africa' beats the refrain.

'It's a strange breeze that blows through these parts:
        Poetry of this order is a murderous act.'"

Havana and Miami are unidentical twins, separated by 90 miles of shark-infested subtropical waters. To its admirers, Havana, a ravaged Caribbean beauty, has culture, grace and a history framed by superlative architecture that dates back 400 years. It also has an impressively low level of crime, a literate and reasonably healthy population and a group of professional architects, planners, historians and conservationists working hard to save it from physical and commercial destruction.

Miami has crime in gory bucketloads, more vice than Havana (as yet), illiteracy, racial tension, cable TV, little modern history (the Wagner House, Lummus Park, is the oldest in Miami-Dade County, dating from 1858), guns, narcotics by the armful and more property development than you can shake a stick at.

Jonathan Glancey, 'The Guardian Newspaper', January 11th 1999.

The Rebel Radio Diary

To a very special Island, its struggles,
history, sounds, beauty and aspirations

...message begins...sent from havana to london agreed stop by our man of international intrigue...

The Rebel Radio Diary

Introduction: In Preparation and Why?

I studied Hispanic Literature at postgraduate level before completing an MPhil in Modern Poetry. My thesis, through criticism and poetry of the Caribbean, was based on the concept of 'Belonging' and 'Spaces': as Barbadian poet Edward Braithwaite writes in the concluding lines to his New World Trilogy 'The Arrivants', 'making/with their/rhythms some—/thing torn/and new'.

We are made aware that there is a creative intention/tension within these lines – the 'making' and 'rhythms', along with a sense of independence – 'their'. But there is also the sense of damage, of some form of fracture and of loss: the 'new' must emerge out of something 'torn'.

I read books by Cuban writers on music, arts and Cuban history, dating back to the arrival of the very first Europeans and rapidly developed a passion for this exciting Caribbean Island. Intrigue and revolution seem as much a part of the culture as sunshine and colour.

October 8th 1997 was the thirtieth anniversary, since his death in combat, of Cuba's adopted and much loved revolutionary hero, Che Guevara. I learned that Che Guevara was not solely charged on gunpowder. He was also a doctor, a writer, a military strategist, philosopher and the man responsible for wiring up a radio transmitter on the Revolution's frontlines. On February 24th 1958, in the Sierra Maestra Mountains to the Northwest of Santiago de Cuba, Che installed his soft weapon against

Capitalism, 'Radio Rebelde'. Broadcasting across Cuban air waves allowed Che to deliver his speeches and the principles of the Revolution direct to the ears of the people.

Music was also broadcast on Radio Rebelde so as to make the point that this Revolution was about 'Socialismo con pachanga' – 'Socialism with rhythm'. Music is, and was then, a fundamental ingredient in the struggle as the Cuban nation has a musical soul.

Together with Up, Bustle and Out, I released an extended-play single in memory of Che and his radio station. Distribution was worldwide and the press reaction was positive, not cynical, as I had feared. There were no captions reading 'The Revolution will now be commercialized!' Indeed, the opposite occurred, to the point where The Guardian Newspaper ran a full-length feature on Che and his life, including a small paragraph about our project. The Performing Rights Society also ran an informative feature in their Statement magazine.

Up, Bustle and Out embarked on a World tour to promote Radio Rebelde, kicking off on the 8th of October 1997, the very day Che Guevara's remains were finally laid to rest in a mausoleum in Santa Clara, Cuba. The Cubans made him a saint – 'San Ernesto de Cuba' – and gave him a state burial. On October 8th we were performing live on stage in Tokyo, Japan and later broadcasting our reason for being there across the Eastern city on Shibuya FM.

The Rebel Radio tour generated interest from East to West, packing out concert halls and clubs before terminating on Italian national TV. We had made money from record sales, merchandise and the tour – capital which was to be reinvested into Radio Rebelde, now Cuba's national radio station and located in Calle 23, Vedado, Havana. I communicated via the Internet with the Director of Radio Rebelde, Señor Mario Robaina Díaz. Together we finalized an exciting musical project.

I was given a list of equipment to purchase for the radio station, ranging from computer paraphernalia to DAT recorders, while Señor Díaz organized a recording studio. I envisaged recording with Cuban Maestros, producing the music, licensing these recordings from them and later releasing them on two Master Session Series albums, along with my own music written and produced in Bristol, UK. The caption by which the product was to be marketed was 'The smokeyness of Bristol, the coolness of Havana'.

During the months of preparation (obtaining a journalist visa, purchasing equipment etc.), I came into contact with many more people who took an avid interest in this project: my record label, Ninja Tune, for one. After hearing our new songs and ideas, they offered to contribute towards the costs of the recording masters. This money was to be spent obtaining studio master tapes of the Cuban Descarga, which is a heavily percussive free-style form of Latin jazz.

I then received a timely call from a young Jules Elvins of Waldo Films, London, requesting the use of our released music for a short film he was making. The conversation turned to Cuba and he found himself on a weekend train to Bristol. We discussed the project in detail, downed bottles of red wine, tampered with rum, smoked cigars and grooved the weekend away in several low-key Bristol hip-hop/funk cellars.

Jules decided to be on board and two days later he rang with the news that, through sponsorship, he had secured 80 minutes of 16 mm film. He was preparing to make a film and a CD-ROM to accompany our releases. We now needed microphones, power and personal belongings. I knocked together a transformer to boost the mains power from 110 volts to 240 volts and encased it in cardboard with Gaffa tape. Into the rucksack it all went, and we were ready to go.

The adventure had advanced to the next stage. It was a stage that did have preconceptions and a philosophy presupposed through education, previous travel, books and Western press. Memories of Latin America flooded back to me. In 1994, I had hacked my way through semi-jungle in Southern Bolivia so that I could follow the final route taken by Che Guevara before he met his fate in a dusty dwelling known as Vallegrande. It was a hell of a place for a romantic revolutionary to have been murdered: a nothingness, a no-man's land, yet somehow fitting for a man who lived by his convictions and died fighting for the integrity of small developing nations and for the demise of imperialism.

The men of imperial power of that time, hoping that Che would be quickly forgotten, buried him in a concealed mass grave under a dirt airstrip, but even in death Che is held in awe. His myth became a tragic blend of woven poetry and harsh reality. It must be stressed that Che did shoot to kill. He had a strong aversion for his enemy and sentenced them to the firing squad once captured and tried. He despised money – Capitalism – yet by some uncanny irony his image has also become one of the most widely exploited selling points.

In Latin America during the 1990s, I witnessed what Che Guevara had witnessed in the 1950s – a continent seeping in poverty. The tin mines in Potosí, Bolivia are the most palpable example of covert imperialism that I encountered. These mines have been exploited since mineral wealth was discovered and extracted by the Spaniards throughout the 16th and 17th centuries. The mines soon will have passed their workable life. Today the mountain is riddled with desperate galleries propped up by precarious timber shoring. There is no electric lighting but plenty of activity from the miners, many of whom are children, working barefoot and without sufficient protection, clothing or tools. The profits from the mines go to foreign businesses. And this is going on in the final years of the millennium and beyond.

So at this extreme of a continent's struggle, I marvelled at Cuba and its Revolution. It has a gritty voice that is shouting out to the rest of Latin America to stand up and resist foreign dependency. It's a country whose fight inspires not only the World's poor but equally leading academics like Jean Paul Sartre, who wrote about it, visited Cuba and termed Che Guevara as 'the most complete man of his age'. Cuba has also attracted the respect and attention of President Nelson Mandela. It is a country of Heroes and Heroines of Worthy Resistance.

In my country, the UK, there is certainly no place for heroes in contemporary society. President Castro has been preyed-upon by the media, the most recent example being during Pope John Paul II's visit to the Island. I do not deny that issues must have been raised which discomfited the Socialist government – but the reporting was flawed in so many aspects, principally by negating history. I still believe (and I hope this will be the case after my trip) that the majority of Cubans will not want to see their Island return to being a backyard for criminal Miami.

That chapter in Cuban history must surely have been read and understood by all.

Obviously, there has rarely been a simple case of right or wrong during the course of any revolution. The hundreds of thousands of Cubans who left for the USA can't all 'be wrong'. Che Guevara said that 'the Cuban Revolution wasn't ever going to be won with elegance'. Perhaps the reality of war was an underlying factor for this mass exodus, along with a Communist outcome. Nonetheless, Che's speech pronounces:

... for all the other countries in the World who are fighting for their freedom against the forces of oppression, we are a lighted torch. Any victory against imperialism is our victory, just as any defeat, is our loss.

Cuba adopted this international stance by becoming a country that, during the 1960s and 70s, exported revolutionaries to other countries to fight oppression. They were the first foreign troops from a developing country to oppose and deal a heavy blow on South Africa's Apartheid regime – a victory that was praised throughout the developing World. Of the 36,000 Cuban troops fighting in Angola over 2000 lost their lives. This is something President Nelson Mandela never forgot. In July 1991 he arrived on the Island to salute the Cuban people and to pay his respects.

I think it is fair to say that the Cuban Revolution was supposed to signify 'independence' at both national and international levels. The 'Bearded Revolutionaries' were the latest hope in Cuba's long struggle for independence. I must now see for myself the way of life in Cuba, push aside, as much as possible, all the preconceptions and discover the spirit of the land. I hope to learn of old and new aspirations, the fears of change and the lives of people in one of the last surviving Socialist bastions of this century, where the President has had over 40 years of unchallenged power.

The Rebel Radio Diary is an emotional and often direct observation, intending also to be historical, humorous, real, fantastical, romantic and, above all, captured through the Aperture of Youth.

The Departure Date is Set

Getting into Cuba with a journalist visa has not been an easy task. It has, however, proved eventful and involved a lot of phone calls among the various departments of the Cuban Embassy in London and Havana. I needed this visa in order to enter Cuba with microphones, DAT recorders, tapes and the 16 mm reels of film and equipment. I will be recording eight songs in Havana which are to be included with the twelve that I have produced and mastered in Bristol before setting off. If I was to have these master tapes confiscated by Cuban officials while leaving the country then two albums and an exciting project would ultimately have been lost.

My contact at Radio Rebelde, whom I know only through our letters and e-mail messages, is Mijail Arteaga, who also runs a 1950s-style recording studio. The sound that came out of his studio set a precedent, along with Havana's Egrem Studio. He always begins his news with a line of poetry 'Good morning from the Island of sun who has suffered tempestuous moments of late' - proof indeed that the weather is a common source of conversation for all cultures. A good start.

A week prior to my departure date he informs me who the musicians are going to be. Richard Egües is Cuba's premier flautist. He will also be my co-arranger and artistic director. The double-bass player will be Gonzalo Noroña, whose lineage boasts some of Cuba's best double-bass players from countless generations. His inspirations are the Cachao family, who put the Cuban Descarga to the World during the 1950s. Indeed these musicians, several of whom, are now in their 70s form part of a generation that set the ground rules for Cuban Salsa as we know it today. Havana is home to this rare collection of vintage jazz musicians. I couldn't be blessed with a greater opportunity, although I want a newer sound with a greater emphasis on tough-tight rhythms and dope hook lines. It all begins on April 7th, when I shall arrive at José Martí International Airport, Havana.

Richard Egües rang me up several days before I left. He spoke in a strong Havana dialect, cutting short words ending in 's', just like the Andalucíans. His voice was deep and gentle, with a Latin rhythm. I syncopated my ears and mind to his timing and realized he was discussing the project. He had started rehearsing and structuring the songs according to our musical preferences. I love bringing dance floors to life, so the genre would have to be the Descarga. Such percussive weight slapped from wooden congas, ringing timbales and cowbells with an undercurrent of sweeping double bass all constitute a powerful Descarga. This is the sole means by which this project can and will, talk a rebel's talk. It needs to so that it will not be surpassed by the wildest redefinitions of the instrument in today's music. In short, we don't want to leave dance floors sterile either today or tomorrow.

It was understood that we were going to record ten songs in eight days. Among all the percussive anarchy, Richard sought a contrast by performing one lighter romantic number, an idea which would embed dynamics into the project. Mijail had booked the studio from April 10th for ten hours per day. The final sound for cutting onto vinyl/CD would be reminiscent of the 1950s, when musicians flitted round the national hotels that were illicitly managed by Italian and Miami gangsters, but with a rougher edge. This dissipated exciting scene all came to an end in 1959 when the Revolutionaries triumphed.

The commercial releases are backed by Ninja Tune Records and will comprise of two Master Sessions albums, each one containing six/seven of our songs, four by the Richard Egües Orchestra, one ambient recording made somewhere in Cuba, and 20 minutes of film footage on CD-ROM format. The idea of the CD-ROM is so that we can film exclusive and original footage of the life and soul of contemporary Cuba. Shooting on 16 mm and Super 8 is an expensive cost to add to this project, but a major priority. I feel it important to portray, through a popular medium, the lives of people in a country famous for its music, spirit, coolness, romantic heroes, beaches, cars, cocktails, cigars, topography and colours...

The project has to generate enough interest to guarantee that this Rebel Radio station continues to transmit beyond the year 2000. Our donations and continued interest should go some

direction of another officer who unloaded the boxes onto various tables in the airport corner. Boycie had been right: he did know 'the whole show'. They took every box apart and started a lengthy bureaucratic process. Bar codes, serial numbers, colours and packaging were all entered on some aged official manuscript. I was given a copy and led to the exit where my contact from Radio Rebelde was waiting for me. He was tired after a long wait. The boxes stayed behind under the understanding 'To be collected upon further instruction'.

Mijail Arteaga had no problems in distinguishing me – I was the last person to pass through the exit doors and he was the only person left in the exit hall. He led me to a beat-up green Jeep. I got behind to jump-start it, as the starting motor had died 15 years previously. The roar from the engine shook the axles, making a disturbing rattle, like when a teenager kicks a can along a dank city street. We drove into the night, into Havana.

April 9th

Today we negotiated a lift to Richard Egües' house with Mijail's neighbour. Here we discussed the artistic direction and recording schedule. We arrived in a Chevrolet - a rusty old glimmer in Havana's streets. Richard occupied the principal spot in his front room, dressed in the classic jazz musician's style – a clean Guayabero shirt and cream linen trousers. His smile was beaming and his aura distilled a lazy peace, the kind of chilled-out nature people seem to achieve as they get older. I shook his huge unsteady hands with the kind of respect due to a maestro of 74. The personal contact resulted in a smile and the offer of a glass of rum – my first in Cuba, and at 10 in the morning!

'Listen to my new recordings, all Descargas.' Richard pressed the play button on his reel-to-reel machine and the music filled the open plan rooms.

'That's exactly what I was hoping for – free rhythm driven inspired jazz.'

'Bueno, that's what you'll get.'

Richard rose to his feet and began shuffling his feet to his music.

'I've played with the best and still I'm respected musically the World over. Last year the Selmer factory invited me to Paris. I played my flute during a magical evening and my heart tells me that I stole the show.'

He ran his fingertips over his crisp shirt collars and returned to his seat. He folded his hands and said, 'I'm proud to be part of your project. This is why I put my name to it. As Cubans we do music for love, money is a side issue. It has to be. Our greatest potential market is closed to us. I live modestly.'

He was, of course, referring to the US market. I had a feeling that this issue would be raised a great number of times during my stay and by a vast cross-section of society.

'I prefer to leave the negotiations to Guillermo.'

I had been clocking this other lanky chap out of the corner of my eyes since I'd arrived. His hospitality was a little forced. He was preoccupied with the business side of our project. After a short discussion we agreed our economic interests, musical objectives and the fee, and we all shook hands. I said to Richard, 'The studio goes out at 30 dollars an hour. We'll work between eight and ten hours per day and the project should be wrapped up in approximately ten days. I pay the studio fees, which are a separate issue from the fees for the rights to the recorded music. I pay you 12,000 dollars for eight song titles. The music will be released commercially by Ninja Tune Records, London who will be able to exploit the master recordings in any way that they see fit.'

'Agreed. And we start on the tenth.'

We shook hands again, drank another rum cocktail before heading off for the Sonocaribe Studio, where the music was to be recorded. It was now almost 11.30 am.

Rene, the patron of Sonocaribe, a state-run recording studio in Vedado, Havana, gave me a tour of the studio. The live room looks like a theatre, with a grand stage and numerous rows of public seating. At the rear of the stage are three live cubicles with windows permitting clear vision between the musicians. The studio equipment is professional, some of it dating from the 1950s, some from the 1990s. It is housed on an upper level that overlooks the whole of the stage and recording cubicles. Rene printed a contract out, confirming hourly rate and recording schedule. The price was favourable because of the nature of our project and our solidarity with Cuba.

Next door to Sonocaribe, within the same building, is Radio Rebelde. Mijail led me to the air-conditioned office of Robaina Díaz, the station director. On the wall there was a wonderful black-and-white blown-up photo of Che Guevara, giving the room a sense of revolutionary pride. Robaina Díaz is also a man of pride. He shook my hand firmly before offering me a seat. He spoke little, but his words were selected so that every one counted.

'Radio Rebelde is Cuba's national radio station. We broadcast the principles of a Revolution that every one of us has inside. News, sport and Cuban music are broadcast 24 hours a day, all year round. We even have listeners in Scotland on short wave. We thank you for your donations and for forming this union with us. You will be welcomed and looked after in all your needs – just address them to Mijail or to me.'

Together they took me on a tour of the station. Radio Rebelde still broadcasts music recorded on 6800 1/4" tapes – because of the lack of CDs and CD players. The reel-to-reel machines are Hungarian and very heavy-looking. The station has 99,000 song titles, of which 70% is Cuban and 30% foreign. It is Cuba's principal transmitter occupying 40 frequencies on the FM dial around the Island. I brought them two broadcasting CD players and over 300 CDs, donated by record companies across the UK, the rest of Europe and Japan. This should add a new musical angle to the station's output.

Having concluded business and formal greetings, I went into Old Havana - La Habana Vieja, now designated a World Heritage Site by UNESCO. I could hear salsa being performed in the bars. It was a glorious sun that illuminated the narrow streets of the once-colonial Spanish Havana. One colour reflected another: yellow, orange, red and sandy stone. It is a perfect setting for a 1950s Chevrolet to roll by or for admiring the coquette skip of an elegant mulatta making her way along this historical backdrop. Cafés line the streets and the lustre and bustle gives rhythm to a lazy afternoon.

Old Havana's culminating point is the Plaza de Armas. Here there are many street stalls selling books, particularly by or on Che Guevara or Fidel Castro. Also for sale are wood carvings of Cuban people, Santería religious symbols, photos and general tourist merchandise. On a stroll, my attention was caught by a magnificent palace with a marble statue of a man in the internal courtyard. Below him was a semicircle of young girls playing classical orchestral music. The palace is now the city museum. I went up to the surrounding balcony, found a sunny spot and let myself drift away on the current of music and the sun. I stayed to admire the 17th century Spanish architecture, the palm trees and the potted garden of the internal plaza. A peaceful solitude swept over me. Thus I stayed for two hours.

Once back on the streets I was in a semi-reverie. I sat on a ground stone below the window of the palace to make more entries in my diary.

A Night with Good Rogues

I had only just started writing when the first rogue came up to me asking if I would like to purchase a box of Romeo and Julieta cigars. Clandestinely, of course.

'Please leave me to write,' I said.

I noticed that he had a kind look and disposition. I have been in many situations like this in a handful of countries: if I wanted to carry on writing, then I would have to walk away; if I hung about, I'd have to talk. It was at this moment that a dancing apparition appeared in front of me – a mulatta asking if I 'wanted anything'. She asked this while rolling her body backwards, forwards and sideways in front of me. An enchantress, who reminded me of the Spanish Gypsy in Laurie Lee's novel 'As I Walked Out One Midsummer Morning'. Lee's character was as taken as I was by such provocation. The mulatta danced those very words written in Lee's novel:

Because how romantic I am. How just poetic. I am for nothing but the heart, you know.

Her friend, up to similar trickery, looked on – jaded for today. Everything about her suggestiveness was impure beauty and demanded personal strength not to be whisked away to some back room of a decaying colonial house in Old Havana to become enwrapped in her rolling movements. It was at this moment that the fourth good rogue stopped in front of me. She was a small frail and lovable old lady asking if I wanted to purchase a bar of soap that she was clutching in her twiggy hands. It was obvious that the soap was a mere pretence. This señora was lonely and passing her early evening in the streets looking for some companionship.

'Are you Spanish, chico? My parents were Spanish, Papa

from Madrid, Mama from Andalucía. I'm pure Cuban and from the heart. I love to dance, to chat – live life to the full. What's your name? I can be your abuelita, if you wish.'

So my 'little grandmother' entered into the circle of good rogues. Each of us had a means of hustling, we all had a different story to recount and we all understood each other from the outset. I've always preferred the clandestine and slightly law-unto-themselves eccentric World. I fell in love with people's bandits in my infancy. The beautiful mulatta appeared to be temporarily put out in front of the old lady, but she soon began her erotic dancing again. Abuelita smiled at me and made a sweeping gesture with her wrist, as if to express all our thoughts for us: 'She's too hot, too beautiful.'

'Fiesta, fiesta,' shouted out Abuelita. We all seemed pleased at this idea and so I took them for a cocktail. When we entered a bar nobody raised an eyebrow, as if this kind of social entourage was an ordinary crowd here. Five cuba libres were brought over to our table and we all introduced ourselves at the toast. The Cuban cigar seller was called Marco, the mulatta Dayami, and her friend Madeleina. Abuelita had the grand title of Margarita de Castro. We drank three or four rum cocktails each while a strange and discommodious seedy atmosphere evolved around us.

The seediness was created by middle-aged, mostly European, men entering with gorgeous young Cuban girls, some of whom appeared to be younger than 16! Once the sun has set, vices seep from out of the historical stonework.

I have never taken much notice of colour and age differences before, but these were contrasts taken to uncomfortable extremes. It was like a book that was as old as time and yet still it didn't read easily. Prostitution is a muddy taboo. The Cuban situation, however, is a little clearer to define. Here we have a society somewhat broken down by a cruel economic blockade. The young girls are well educated but what can they do or have in life on a very basic salary that is paid in Cuban pesos? Many of the cafés, shops, nightlife and 'nice' things to be had in life when you are growing up are labelled in US dollars. I am not putting forward a justification of their actions, merely an explanation. It discomfited me to see such young girls, of unique beauty and intelligence, selling desperate sex in such a controversial manner.

The question really is, In a society of economic justice, would many of these girls be doing this? I bet the answer is a palpable NO. A crime, of sorts, is therefore being committed. I believe that these seedy base European men are culpable: almost all are past their sell-by date, and probably married. Their power 'to have' is sadly embodied in money and in a country's suffering. They know that fresh green dollar bills can buy them sprightly beauty that otherwise they would be incapable of getting on their own merit or charm. The Cuban term for the Island's prostitution phenomenon is Jinetería, and it is recognized by the Revolution as one of the results of the economic blockade.

I paid the bill and we left. Margarita de Castro suggested that we go to her house and drink more rum. Margarita lives in a wonderful colonial house that, in its day, must have been home to a family of wealthy merchants. It is close to the Old Havana's port entrance situated on the famous street Calle Obispo. The whole barrio evokes a feeling of a past era that was once decorated with extravagant constructions, merchants trading, dockyard activity, markets, shops and a lively street culture.

Today, the markets, shops and people are still there. Slowly the houses are being renovated with funds from the World Heritage. Some day all the façades of this barrio will be touched up and restored to their previous dusky glory. For the time being, Margarita is one of the many Cubans who live in a splendid decadence. Her doors are huge and the windows open onto stone balconies that overlook the street and all its activities. The street ambience fills the rooms like a lively recording. The ceiling is church-like and decorated in finest plasterwork. Columns break up the living space and the floor is tiled with painted ceramics that would fetch a tidy price in an English antique shop. In short, Margarita's domain is a tarnished portrait of an extravagance that could only have come from a period when wealth and growth were in their prime: a merchant's show of success.

I took my leave of her, promising that she would be seeing me again soon. Marco said his farewells and Dayami decided that she would accompany me all the way to the bus stop. Crossing the plaza, I sensed the stillness of the night. Havana seemed to close in on us. The sea lapped at the old port walls as if trying to tell me a secret. The buildings became obscure forms and the night's stars winked at us. Dayami took my hand and I felt encouraged to take her by the waist and perform a few salsa steps with her. We danced for half an hour. It was an affectionate finish to a perfect day with Havana's musical Maestros, Cuba's national radio station and Havana's lovable rogues.

April 10th–22nd

When I arrived at Sonocaribe Studio, it seemed to me that the entire community of Havana's vintage musicians, along with their offspring, were involved in this project. They were setting up their instruments: Richard Egües was tuning his grand piano, the double-bass player was already jamming with the percussionists. The stage activity was a pleasure to watch. I took a back seat to observe the musical habits of these Maestros until Richard spotted me. Before I knew it, I was shaking hands with 15 or so of them. I noticed how they had all preserved a casual coolness with their age. After the handshakes, I got smacks, taps, dancing gestures, jokes and kisses. The friendship was instant and everyone smiled.

The Cuban Maestros who are to be playing on this project and their instruments are as follows:

Richard Egües:
> director/composer/orchestrator/flautist/pianist.

Blas Egües: timbales and cowbell.
Mario Ortega: congas.
Peñalver: Richard's mentor – the man from Havana.
Guido Sarria: congas.
Pedro Ariosa: guiro.
Gonzalo Noroña: double bass.
Vicente Mora: vocals.
Pedro Jiménez: vocals.
Carlos del Valle: vocals.
Pepe Olmo: vocals.
Javier Olmo: vocals.
Esneldo Sánchez: violin.
Jorge Padilla: viola.
Tomás Ibáñez: cello.
Ricardo Egües: flute.
Juan Larrinaga: trumpet.
César López: sax.
Lázaro Hernández: violin.
Manuel López: studio engineer, Sonocaribe
> Estudios.

When they spoke to me, I was riding the waves of a rhythmical Spanish tongue, slow, bouncy and with deep organic tones. Observing the stage taking shape reminded me of why I once chose to be a performing musician, on the road, lugging equipment, long journeys and long nights. It would sound crazy, bizarre to these Maestros to know that I can now earn more money and put in less time by DJing. The live scene is simply where I would prefer to be but high costs prevent it. The feeling of performing together, reading and inspiring each other and causing the dance floor to erupt is a stimulant that makes it all worth while. The fleeting comments that jumped between the musicians, the laughter, the tuning of instruments, all go to make up these magical moments. It was the start of a new project, music in a new context, and in this studio we had brought together a scene with vibes that would stretch a long way.

The days have rolled by in the studio. The vibes are still with us. I love the clothes these Maestros wear, true to the stereotypical image. Richard is always impeccably dressed in white flannel or linen trousers, light leather shoes and a laced Guayabero shirt. He's a gentleman, what the Spanish call a caballero. All the Maestros wear well-pressed shirts and flannel trousers. Some sport shades and Panama hats. They love to smoke and drink. Several of the cheekier band members have discreetly inquired about me purchasing a bottle of rum. At the beginning, Richard had instructed me not to do this. The mixing of spirits and music is a combination he is over familiar with – he told me how previous recordings have been abandoned due to drunken amusements. Of course, he smiled when reflecting upon his memories then said, 'But this can't happen now. When the songs are mastered, we will have a fiesta in my casa.'

After one recording session, I was offered clandestine Punch cigars by a friend of Mijail's. I bought a beautiful box of 25 fat Habanos for $20. A box of Habanos has the feel of a special book, a family treasure - something worth loving and time. The decoration is classic, usually dotted with golden intricacies. Lifting the wooden lid of such a treasure chest holds a moment of great expectation, like the great explorers and pirates who came upon illicit booty, all the better being contraband. ¡Qué va!

On peeling back the painted cover, 1 saw slender symbols of Cuba's fashion and history. 1 prefer to believe the myth that they are rolled on the thighs of beautiful mulattas. They smoke better! 1 offered them round. After toking on my first Punch in Cuba, 1 saw the smoke rise like rich castle turrets in the evening sun. Or was it the smoke rising up to the stage spotlights? Or

could it have been a blanket of mist sweeping inland from the sea? Or put more realistically, it could have been smoke from cigars exhaled by 15 musicians. The pleasurable aroma added to this formidable pastime.

It's amazing that such a simple thing as a fat cigar can make one feel invincible, cool and contented. I'd wager that puros were an essential ingredient to the Revolutionaries' victory on January 1st 1959. Cigars enhanced the romantic and mythical status that Castro, along with his band of bearded soldiers, evoked in the eyes of the ordinary Cubans, and of the World at large.

Castro started his Revolution with only 12 surviving men who made it to the refuge of the Sierra Maestra mountain range, Southern Cuba. Twelve men don't win wars. Public support and participation are fundamental to forming a people's army. With quality leadership, intelligence, an appealing image, and a wealth of conviction, one has a formidable force, and Castro had all these qualities. The cigar became a symbol that romantically defined the Revolution and national pride. What I am implying is that, had it not been for the cigar, events might have turned out differently for Cuba's most recent revolutionaries.

Pepe Olmo, one of the vocalists on this record, is also one of Cuba's most famous traditional salsa vocalists. Cheekiness and good humour are dominant features of his character, and, like all the Maestros, he takes to people quickly. He stood proudly on the stage, wearing glasses and clutching his lyric sheets. We all looked down from the studio console. The stage was vast – he looked as if he was standing in a desert. The sweetness of his voice and lyrics sounded more impressive when the air vibrated up from the back of his throat. His voice is a cultural inheritance that has matured from years of smoking and shouting in order to be heard among the crowds in concert halls. That and the rum.

During his vocal delivery his facial expressions told a biographical story. Pepe is a man who has charmed many girls with his sonnets and his cheeky nature. He once knew the ecstasy of amour and the tragedy of loss. His musical history reminded me of a cask of sherry: the longer the sherry stays in the barrel, the more it impregnates the wood, and this browned mature liquid is later bottled with a sweet rich organic flavour. Such refining has no shortcuts: he has paid his dues on the long road to becoming el número uno.

In Latin music, like the Hip-hop/Latin/Jazz/World-Funk fusion I play and write, the unsung heroes are the rhythm section. They are fundamental, ensuring that the tempo remains as tight throughout the song so that the soloists can wander. On these Latin songs, the rhythm comes courtesy of the guiro, cowbell, timbales, congas and double bass. Latin rhythms have an emphasis known as the efecto, which is a means of signifying a change in the song or of sparking off new life into the proceeding section. The rhythm locks and the notes of the drums tap out a melody between the high and low drums. The cowbells, timbales and congas are played between the low and high notes simultaneously.

The guiro is the strangest instrument in this collection. It fills the rhythm out, occupies a continual space and provides a subliminal repetition. Its importance is therefore paramount. Yet, this instrument is ridiculously simple. The guiro player stands for hours stroking a stick along a serrated edge of hollow wood. I think a guiro player has to have a certain type of personality, a certain craziness, like a drummer who beats the hell out of skins for hours in a room, ears ringing upon re-entering the outside World. In Cuba, you are better off being a guiro player than many other professional state-run and state-paid jobs. The guiro player gets to travel the World stroking his wooden shell to packed-out concert halls.

The Cubans tell this guiro story. The Director of an orchestra is recording an album in Havana. When the recordings are completed, he goes to mix the songs at a different studio, where he is told that they are one channel short on the mixing table. Something has to give in order to mix all the instruments. The studio engineer says to the director, 'The best option is to take out the guiro.'

The director replies, 'No, you can't take out the guiro. Absolutely not, I played it.'

After one recording session I sauntered down to Old Havana to take some historical air. I called by Margarita de Castro's house. She was expecting me,

'Roody, listen to this.'

She pressed Play on an enormous ghetto-blaster and crackles emanated from a wooden speaker fixed precariously to the wall. 'This is Havana,' I figured. 'Nothing works perfectly, but things do work in a roundabout manner.'

Margarita fumbled with the leads and a Latin House song emerged from the crackling cones. She smiled and started grooving like a prop for a video for Kool and the Gang's 'Funky Granny'. That over, she brought up the subject of Dayami.

'A lovely girl, muy caliente, a great dancer and, of course, extremely naughty. Lots of naughty girls in Havana.'

I was beginning to take strongly to my Cuban grandmother. She was real, of a curious nature, and always ready for fun.

'You'll see her again, then?' she inquired, a sparkle in her eye.

'I'm not sure, Margarita. We'll see.'

We were standing on her balcony, looking out over one of the busiest streets in Havana.

'Not much has changed here in my time,' she contemplated. 'It has always been an active street like this: people, shops, families selling bits and bobs, lovers kissing in doorways. A

TV crew came here once from London to film from my balcony. Rich air this is, Roody, and beautiful it feels inside.'

I bid Margarita good night and closed the door behind me. The wind had picked up and the temperature had dropped by several degrees. I looked down calle Obispo towards the port and saw Dayami in a nearby doorway. She had spotted me on Margarita's balcony and was waiting for me on this tempestuous evening in Havana. She looked like a Cuban midnight pearl, iridescent with every motion, with a flower in her hairgrip and glossy red lipstick. I offered her my arm and looked up to the blackened, magical and tormented sky. As the wind ripped round Havana's harbour and the sea sent spray onto the pavements, we strolled along, accompanied by a grand moon.

I returned home on the Camello, a stretched bus shell pulled by a lorry cabin. Because this is a very cheap form of travel and everyone pays in Cuban pesos, the Camello is always full. Transport is one of the most pressing problems of the Special Period, announced by President Castro in 1991, because of the shortage of fuel. Cuba has to import fuel, even though it has refineries, because the oil grade is too low for mechanical engines and the cost of upgrading is prohibitive. I got on at the last stop before the Camello passes through the tunnel leading to East Havana. It was ram-jammed, but everyone squeezed together to let me on. The doors closed with a hair's-breadth to spare.

A señora next to me informed me from the corner of her mouth that I had lipstick on my cheeks, like patches of touching-up paint on a Chevrolet's front wing panel. I spent the journey trying to find the elbow room to rub it off.

One day at the studio, I announced to the Maestros that my campañero, Jules, would be with us the following day to begin filming. These humble characters began to flutter.

'Filmado. ¡No me digas! ¡Van a filmar!

They began to look critically upon themselves and their

dress.

'Oh, these shoes, they're naff, shoddy old things.'

'Best dig out my favourite old shirt.'

'Not that one you used to wear at the Tropicana?'

'I love it, tío. ¿Qué problema tienes?'

'My wife has made me some new trousers.'

'I'll have to wear my shades and hat.'

'Oh, por Dios, they're going to film us.'

We all vacated the studio, with the usual laughs and jokes about what the evening had in store for us. Mijail and I went to the car compound in search of transport in which to pick Jules up from the airport. The only vehicle available was a rough-and-ready camouflage Jeep with 'RADIO REBELDE' painted on the side in blood-red. It must have been a Comandante's Jeep at some time. It was the perfect vehicle in which to welcome Jules to Havana. The obstacle – there is always an obstacle in Cuba – was getting it fired up. The bonnet was propped up and we dropped a battery in from another vehicle. Mijail whacked the contact leads on with a wooden baton and the Old Boy of the Revolution spluttered into existence again. We were on the road.

Jules's first impressions of Havana were positive. He marvelled at the architecture and chuckled when a Chevrolet 'Verde y Blanco' rolled by. He was surprised at the stylish dress and cleanliness of the people. To be honest, I think he was a bit blown away by it all, being a well-to-do arty lad from London. That evening, the Cuban family we were staying with had prepared lobster for us. Their neighbour had plucked the lobsters from the sea that very afternoon. We cracked open the Cristal beer cans and dined the evening away in a room overlooking the sea.

In the studio, the Maestros came and went as each one completed his session. By the halfway mark, we had four days to add the final link in the chain, mixing the songs. Richard was living up to his musical reputation. While observing him conduct a four-piece string ensemble, I realized more than ever that this was a maestro who lived and breathed music. Richard views the World in a musical context; his life like a short story that begins and finishes with a treble clef. Everything in between reads of a life interpreted through sweet melodies and long nights behind grand pianos.

His blood sings in his offspring as well. They are all accomplished musicians in their own right. His son Ricardo was also a musical director as well as a flautist. From the studio console he communicated bar numbers and efectos to the musicians in their pans while they recorded. He played the role of team coach, instructing them, inspiring them, keeping them together and disciplining them in bar lengths. Like his father, he was a man of few words, but his friendship and warmth were sincere.

The early evenings were still spent walking curiously along the streets discovering Havana, only now we were filming on 16 mm and Super 8. On discovering an interesting hive of activity, we would stop, Jules would set up his cameras and shoot reels of film. To avoid any unwanted confrontations with the police, Robaina Díaz was trying to get us 'all-areas' visas, which would mean free access throughout Cuba. This involved telephone conversations, meetings, payments and much paperwork. He assured us that, by hook or by crook, we would be awarded this authority. It was simply a cat and mouse game until the Word was given. From Above.

We had to become real tourists at some stage and Jules had the perfect scenario planned. One afternoon we sauntered into Old Havana and drank Mojito rum cocktails at La Bodeguita del Medio, a bar just up from Havana's cathedral, made famous because Ernest Hemingway used to frequent it. Latin-American enthusiasts might be more impressed by the fact that Chile's old

Marxist President, Dr Salvador Allende, drank here on several occasions during the rebel climate of the 1960s and Castro himself has let loose, downed rum and smoked his Cohiba cigars in this historic little watering hole.

Passing Entry

Robaina Díaz sent a late fax to the Cuban Embassy in London requesting a press visa for Jules. Prior to his departure, Jules had been turning up at the Embassy at 9 am every morning to try to procure such a visa, to no effect. In the end, he purchased a tourist visa from a back-street agency and entered Cuba with three professional film cameras – not an ideal situation. A fax from London had since been received at Radio Rebelde, asking after Jules' whereabouts and what he intended to film. We were asked to present ourselves at a Government press office in Havana to register our movements. Robaina Díaz has composed a letter in support of Jules' journalist status. The catch in this bureaucratic riddle is that Jules was expected to pay a further $120 for this pleasure. Furthermore, we were required to give regular information on our movements to provincial government offices.

We decided to ignore the whole scenario of reporting to provincial government offices. From now on we were living like real Cubans, with one foot in the dark, the other in the light. We pretended to be photographic and film enthusiasts, making a tourist film to show our friends and boast about how great Cuba is.

Another Passing Entry

Cuba, I feel, is controlled by a state engine that treads heavily on the brakes while one is freewheeling. One just doesn't have the feeling of total freedom of movement. The Spanish novelist Miguel De Cervantes wrote in Don Quixote de la Mancha, 'Liberty is the greatest gift bestowed upon man by a divine god.' I believe so strongly in the word 'freedom' and all that it entails. There are simply too many police here, too many rules, too many officially dressed people clutching clipboards. Inevitably, there are too many people ducking and diving under this social order. Just occasionally, I sense a paranoia in the air and I've yet to work out why. However, it is not as though I have to look over my shoulder at any time.

It was a peaceful evening when I sat on the harbour wall, with a midnight moon lurking over El Morro castle in the distance. El Morro was built to protect Havana, principally from English pirates, who sacked the city on several occasions, escaping with hulls full of gold. In reality, what was going on was a bandit's code of conduct: the Spaniards stole the gold from the indigenous peoples and then the English pirates were guilty of receiving stolen property, robbery and double handling. It all

evened out in the end – for the Europeans. The Spaniards built fortifications to protect their interests. The English pirates and merchants either endeavoured to break through these citadels or sailed upon other oceans in search of fresh adventures. Maybe this tale unveils the origin of the Spanish proverb:

A thief who robs a thief is granted a hundred-year pardon.

Cuba is a hot country and this is reflected in the clothing. The Cubans are a handsome people and the girls have a particular brand of beauty that is enhanced by light clean garments and mountains of vitamin E. They have rhythm, and a natural coquettish nature, both flirtatious and charming. This flirtatiousness comes as a cultural shock to visitors from colder climes, and you do find yourself succumbing to 'having a look'. However, I noticed that it wasn't just me that would stop and turn to watch a señorita walk past. The Cuban men do it too.

The music house, La Casa de la Trova, is well worth a visit in any city. In Central Havana, it is a glorious colonial house, with no expense spared in its construction. Of course, today it is testament to a country that cannot get hold of the materials it needs to fuel its renaissance. Nonetheless, this Casa de la Trova remains inspiring. I entered through a grand wooden door and was met with the melody of a guitar beckoning me in a warm stroking manner. The soft yellow walls, brown frames and coloured-glass windows make this a perfect location for musicians to get up, take centre stage and do their thing for a moment's glory.

When we arrived, a guitar maestro was slumped over his instrument, strumming away as if he was in a half-dream. I noticed that the guitar was amplified with a vocal microphone placed inside the guitar body. The strings must have been stretched to one side to have made this possible. The maestro resembled a classic photo of a Cuban. He was dressed in pale blue jeans, tucked up a good seven inches, and a deep red Latin shirt.

His shirt brought him to life against a whitewashed wall and a black grand piano. He was old and weathered, yet seriously cool, with his image reflected in the piano's tilted lid. You could almost imagine him in his youth, standing by a doorway in Havana, smoking a cigar and running his fingers through his black wavy hair. This man was a professional, and the Casa de la Trova was where it was at for him.

Later he accompanied two older women, who reflected Cuba's history: one was of African origin, the other Iberian. They sang passionate poetry that related to their lives. I remembered Nicolás Guillén's poem 'The Ballad of the Two Grandfathers', in which Guillén wrote rhythmically of his African grandfather hunting the parched plains with a spear, and of his Spanish grandfather chartering new oceans dressed nobly in an explorer's ruff, buying information and services with shiny glass beads.

Another mature lady took centre stage, a mulatta with remarkable finesse. She coiled the microphone lead up while speaking a few introductory words. She looked into my eyes – or so I wished to believe – and began to sing her first line:

> Quiero escaparme con la vieja luna
> (I wish to escape with the old moon)

Her stage presence displayed a magnificent dignity. There was no spotlight upon her; instead, rays of light from the early evening sun penetrated the coloured window glasses and beamed onto the stage. She stepped in and out of the coloured lights. I found myself slipping into the spell that she was casting over us. Her feet swept the floor from side to side and she never lifted her eyes from me. She held the stage with comparative ease. I knew that she had sung like this since her youth. Her body comfortably filled out a long Spanish-style dress. Her high-heeled shoes were red, like her lips and the flower tucked in her hair.

The guitarist plucked the notes, guided by her vocal melodies. He sat cross-legged, strumming dreamy chords that I have not heard since Andres Segovia played Tárrega's composition Recuerdos de la Alhambra during a magical night in the Alhambra gardens, Granada, Spain.

As she left the stage, she passed in front of me. I felt an exciting shiver down my back. Expecting a little flattery for having sung so passionately, she held out her hand and I kissed it.

'Mañana, come by and I'll sing you another.'

This was an invitation too good to refuse. The following day we would be in the studio until the early evening. It struck me that the Casa de la Trova was the perfect place to unwind.

Passing Entry

I was fed up eating pizzas bought on the street for seven Cuban pesos. They were edible... just. Cuban cuisine is nothing to write home about; as a result, I was losing weight fast.

Let me describe Jules. He was an eccentric young gentleman, quite serious for someone of only 25. His sense of humour tickled me, having an edge of cynicism. He expresses himself with sentences of great Old English pomp; his loftiness came from that cliché public schooling that few off us are familiar with, outside period dramas. He peppered his speech liberally with expressions such as 'quite appalling', 'really', 'this is as good as it gets, boy', 'bloody hell, it's a bit of a poor show, rather a shambles if I might say so' and 'he's a right ol' bastard'.

From public school he went to Oxford to study Theology, but abandoned his studies halfway through after his tutor had had a discreet word in his ear. Jules wasn't surprised, as he readily admits to shagging too many women and consuming too much beer and drugs. He was the stereotype of an English art-house film-maker: his hair was thick black, scruffy and curly; his body was thin and his skin pale. When the maestros met him, they amused themselves with jokes about how he needed to be pegged out naked on a washing line for several days so that he could blend in better. To them, he looked ill.

Jules strongly resembled Paul Maghan when he shot Withnail and I, and he must have led a similar lifestyle to the characters in that film. I bet he has rolled a great number of 'Camberwell Carrots' or, in his case, 'Brixton Buffers', and will continue to do so within the confines of his London digs, surrounded by an eccentric arty entourage.

His first comment on arrival was 'This is just so perfect, man', followed by 'I need to get my hands on a box of fat Cohiba cigars before operations begin'. He acquired several boxes via friends of friends. Cuba! From that moment on, I would often see him wearing shades, leaning over his 16 mm camera housed on a tripod, checking out interesting angles and shots. He normally carried a rucksack stuffed with cameras, lenses and other film paraphernalia. Of course, all this weighed in heavy. At the end of a long day, he would often look the worse for wear and would say, 'I think we should call it a day now. I'm really fucked, man.'

He had a fascination for Cuba's coolness which he expressed by exclaiming 'Cool!' every time he spotted something cool, for example when a 1950s Chevrolet rolled along a back street, a Cuban commented on his Cohiba hanging religiously from the corner of his mouth or, he spotted a beautiful building or a mural of Che Guevara.

We instantly got along together. Jules was himself 'cool'.

Graham Greene was one of his literary heroes. Like everyone who comes to Cuba on a mission, he'd read Greene's novel Our Man in Havana. 'Greene's an enigma – an elusive man. One of the 20th century's greatest British novelists. He's just wicked, man –

incredibly cool. He was chums with Che, wrote him a dedication in honour of his presence in the United Nations, if I recall. Che would speak for hours on end at the UN. Greene wrote some brassy paragraph for the man. Something bravado like:

They feared that the echo of his voice would rise up from the audience hall; they were afraid to see the man they hated was loved by the whole World. That fear would later contribute to perpetuate his legend, and bullets can do no harm to a legend.

As an armchair theorist, Jules had potential. One evening, while walking through old Havana, he observed a clock built into the façade of a monumental building.

'Oh, look, it's ten to two in the morning by that clock. Clearly it's only about eight, the evening is young. This is actually a global phenomenon. Incredible amounts of money have been spent on building palatial monuments and churches. All have clocks as their centrepiece and only about five per cent actually work.'

Another theory was about Cuba's stamps:

'Listen to this, man. Have you noticed that it costs 65 centavos to post a card or letter to the USA? All stamps of this value have an image of Che on the front. It's just so cool. It only costs 50 centavos in postage to Europe, which is obviously much further. The CIA are responsible for murdering Che and now the Cubans send Washington a picture of the man they killed with every letter.'

Another theory was about what he was seeing in contemporary Cuba,

'It's, you know, so good what we're doing right now. We're here before Cuba has to change. This is Castro's Revolutionary Cuba and he hasn't got too long before he pops his clogs. What happens next is uncertain. I just don't want to see this country, after defying the USA's imperialist machine and quest for global and moral domination, fall back into the hands of those fuckers. It won't, of this I feel certain. Generations have formed this wonderful Island's identity. Cubans are intelligent enough to let the changes that will inevitably come develop at Cuba's pace. This country is so famous when you think about it. When do you ever hear any news in the papers or on the TV about Portugal, Madagascar or Bolivia?'

'The World secretly admires Cuba for its David-and-Goliath fairy tale. The Rebels won and made a unique global stand opposing Third World exploitation by Western firms and banks. Look at the Russians now, forced onto their knees begging at the World Bank's doors for US dollars. Russia is now yet another country with a noose round its neck, being told what path they must walk by foreigners – a kind of second Africa. Cuba sees the World through a different lens, one that is well focused, but the angle is a little too wide. This is not a narrow-minded country by any means, but its hopes and aspirations are beyond its means for the present. Here, listen, man, I have theories on this political schism, but I fancy a beer. A cool Cristal, if that's all right.'

I was starting to form my own theories on Cuba's political situation. The most important point is that this country has been treated illegally and inhumanely. The USA has enforced a trade embargo on Cuba for nearly 40 years. It also enforces covert policies on other countries that have economic links with Cuba, so that a country that trades with Cuba and also has US interests, for example bank debts, can expect the thumbscrews to be tightened on them too; therefore, most countries stay clear. Upsetting the World's superpower is not a wise course of action if you're poor and dependent on it. Make no mistakes about this – the US embargo affects the lives of ordinary Cubans, who wish to be integrated internationally and on terms of mutual respect.

A great many have fled the Island for the USA, believing

that opportunity awaits them there. Countless mainland Latin Americans attempt to cross the US border, and in far greater numbers, but this isn't talked about or exploited politically, in the same extent as those who cross those troubled Straits of Florida.

Life in the USA can be overwhelming, with language barriers, different systems and loss of cultural identity. I always remember the all-encompassing sadness in Oscar Hijuelos' novel Empress of the Splendid Season. Hijuelos dedicated the novel to the memory of a cleaning lady in New York – a respectable proud señora, once from an upper-class family in Cuba. This novel captures the sadness of displacement and disillusionment and is a narrative of social-historical value.

At the wake of the cleaning lady's husband, who was also Cuban-born, were present his US-born daughter Alicia and her North American husband and children. The daughter says to her children,

'Always remember that your grandfather was Cuban.'

Hijuelos then writes through the voice of Alicia's brother, Rico:

The mystery of that comment, coming as it did from his dear upstate ex-hippie sister Alicia, surprised Rico, who had not thought Alicia particularly aware of her 'Cubanness', and yet he had to admit that, with the room crammed mainly with Cubans and other Latinos of their father's acquaintance, so many of them grief stricken, he had felt a great surge of pride (among many other emotions). He would recall many of his neighborhood friends coming to pay their respects; handshakes, pats on the back. But in general, a great sadness descended upon him; part of the world, a curtain of identity, as it were, had been torn away.

(Empress of the Splendid Season, Bloomsbury, 1999, p 304)

'Making/with their/rhythms some-/thing torn/and new' –
it is a struggle with no clear objective, saturated with enduring
sadness. No dignity either, when a six-year-old Cuban boy who,
having lost his mother in crossing the turbulent Straits, becomes
used as a political possession and stopped from returning, despite
his father's wishes who remains in Cuba. In all the media fuss,
posing with US politicians and Disney figures, sporting a smile as
if he understands all that is going on, his dead mother becomes
some abstract reality. (Plight of Elian González during Dec''99 and Jan'
00).

The embargo has endured for so long, and with the
intention of isolating an entire country, that it has become one of
the century's most calculated crimes against humanity, in my
view. It has been extended to food, clothing and even medicines.
The reasons for such inhumane treatment are probably very
complex, but the World has since learned that dialogue is a far
better way to deal with your neighbour than invasion, seclusion
and aggression.

I may be heavily criticized for this observation, but I can't
help wondering if race has anything to do with this. Cuba is a
predominantly black country. When some of the Revolutionaries
began to arrive in Havana on New Year's Day 1959 (Castro arrived
on 8th January), many of the white upper classes were alarmed to
discover that Cuba was 'so black'. This I read in archives housed in
Havana. My point is, would a principally white country, of direct
European decent, have been isolated from the rest of the World
and deprived of basic amenities for over 40 years? I really do not
think so.

In all tragedies there is irony. The irony here is that the
embargo cruelly defies humanity, yet Cubans display more
humanity and less greed than any other culture that I have come
across.

Cuba's most pressing problems are economic, such as

exports and monetary issues. The coins here have two very different and contrasting sides. One boasts the rebel image of Che Guevara and other revolutionary icons – the peso; the other displays the White House – the dollar. Both currencies exist and both are widely used. Don't take any notice of the guidebooks that deem the Cuban peso useless to tourists. It all depends on how you go about what you do in Cuba.

The Malecón along Havana's seafront on Fridays and Saturdays becomes a weekend mini-fiesta. There are stalls selling food and drinks, all in Cuban pesos. I bought many a beer at this event and in the little villages throughout Cuba's interior. The beer comes in a brown waxed paper cup, in a good half-pint measure. The Cuban men like it too, judging by the numbers queuing and staggering.

In Cojímar, near where Ernest Hemingway lived and developed the idea for The Old Man and the Sea, I paid for everything that I consumed in pesos. When I offered the barman a ten-dollar bill, he blankly refused it. However, the fishermen all round me didn't. One went off to bring me a lobster, while another brought me some massive prawns. Both were for sale in US dollars.

Why do so many people want US dollars? The answer is simple. The Cuban peso can only purchase state-controlled goods, such as select clothing, rice, beans, fruit, vegetables, transport, and cheap drinks. Most other commodities are a luxury to ordinary Cubans and are sold in separate 'dollar shops'. For example, a bottle of Havana Club rum is sold in dollars and goes for export. The state pay is in pesos, at an average of 300 pesos per month. Seventeen dollars won't go far here in a dollar shop.

Cuba's youth are the victims of this system, as Castro's revolution is just another in Cuba's turbulent history to them. It's distressing to sit in a bar, drinking a rum cocktail and smoking a cigar below ceiling fans while lots of young Cubans look in through the patio grills. They are forbidden to enter because the drinks are sold in dollars only. Men and women look expectantly at you in the hope that you might invite them in to join you for a drink.

Castro must be aware that this dual monetary system is encouraging materialism. For this reason, the National Bank has introduced a third currency, the 'convertible peso'. A convertible peso is equal to one US dollar and will hopefully, in the near future, push the US dollar out of the hands of ordinary Cubans. Che Guevara, who loathed money and its effects, was for a period Cuba's Bank Minister. It wasn't long after he'd taken office that he resigned. Some jobs just do not suit certain people's characters.

Another pressing problem is transport. Public transport is incredibly cheap but not all that frequent. I used the Camello and Wah Wah buses (stand-up cheap buses with room for bicycles) for the atmosphere. I enjoyed travelling this way, but I don't have to do it day in, day out. There were times in the evenings when I waited for up to two hours for a bus. By the time the bus arrived, the queue would be extensive. The bus would pull up, seemingly full, and yet somehow everyone managed to get on.

This experience is part of a human puzzle, which contains plenty of magic and mountains of goodwill. The pieces

do fit together somehow. One would have thought that in the early 1990s, when Castro announced the Special Period on the collapse of trade with Russia, Cuba would have sunk shortly after. Why are the Cubans still healthy, well dressed, educated, athletically strong, scientifically, socially and culturally advanced and, more to the point, not starving? The answers lie in understanding Cuba and the fundamental human condition: the will to survive against all odds. The quality of that survival depends on passion and conviction. Cubans have had centuries of struggle; therefore, this is nothing new, nor any more difficult.

April 22nd

Castro's Revolutionary Government, like any government, has introduced sceptical policies. The policy I disagree with most is the curb imposed on university students. Castro himself graduated from Havana University as a doctor of law. Havana's University in Vedado is a grand affair, and beautifully preserved. wide stone stairs lead up to the main entrance. The polished columns and opulent doorway give the impression that you are about to enter a palace. Inside, there is a corridor leading to a busy central plaza. All the various faculty buildings are built round this plaza. It's a hive of activity, and very typical of a rich Spanish university today. Students sit under trees, sharing notes and debating. Books and bags litter the grass, people come and go and young lovers gaze earnestly at one another in the sun.

It was here that I met Ernesto, who had come from Santiago de Cuba to study Language and Literature. His second language was Russian. Lots of Cubans began to study Russian when Cuba began trading and receiving economic investments from the then Soviet Bloc. How strange to hear Latinos in a hot Caribbean setting speaking such an unlikely foreign tongue! Russia sent lots of technicians and engineers, thus beginning a period of development programmes, including bloody powerful missiles.

This bizarre East -West relationship certainly had its ups and downs. Che Guevara would have preferred Cuba to follow China's Communist model, and no government, World power or no, argues with China. Castro wasn't convinced, and sealed links with the Russians. Initially, it showed great promise, and expectations were high. Suffice it is to say that Russia poured vast amounts of capital and technology into Cuba. The Russians probably viewed Cuba as a minor debt, but necessary as a friendly Socialist nation in the Western Hemisphere, and so close to the USA. This generosity inevitably included military arsenal to protect Cuba's independence. Cuba soon built up a massive military machine.

Revolutionary Cuba prioritized defence in order to resist counter-revolutionary movements and CIA-supported invasions from mainland USA. Such a build-up of force by the Russians on a distant small Island was considered dubious by many. Let's not forget that both the USA and Europe have stationed nuclear warheads and missile launchers in countries closer to home, in the middle distance and way off into orbit.

The situation got out of hand in October 1962 when US Intelligence spotted extensive Soviet missile bases under construction in Cuba. On October 16th the CIA announced to President John F. Kennedy that the bases were being stocked with nuclear missiles. The balance was shifting. The Cuban Missile Crisis brought the World to the brink of a nuclear showdown.

Four years prior to this tense historical upset, our hero, Graham Greene, wrote the following in his aforementioned novel:

Number 1 of March 8 paragraph A begins in my recent trip to Santiago 1 heard reports from several sources of big military installations under construction in mountains of Oriente Province stop these constructions too extensive to be aimed at small rebel bands holding out there stop...

So where did Our Man of International Intrigue get his intelligence from before the rest of the World? Some of President Kennedy's hard-line advisers were keen to get the war started, as proven by recently declassified documents. The public release of 'Kennedy's Secret Tapes' revealed a president who was prudent and sensitive to the implications of a nuclear war. He entered into discreet discussions with the Russian Premier Khrushchev down temporary phone lines. Both leaders had been responsible for creating this paranoid Cold War condition but, when it came down to the nitty-gritty, the will simply wasn't there. We all live in hope that lessons were learned.

These secret conversations didn't involve Castro, although the issue took place on Cuban territory. This fact alone highlighted Russia's role in Cuba as being an exterior interest in the Western Hemisphere, and little else.

The mood changed over the years until Castro announced the Special Period in 1991. Russian assistance was no longer forthcoming, owing to the regime's collapse and multiple border and independence wars. Castro considers his lack of foresight in the collapse of the Soviet Bloc to be his gravest error of political judgement. In short, the golden keys to newly found coffers, once opened, were quickly diminished. Cuba was left to stand on its own two feet, surrounded by a trade embargo preventing it from walking. A Special Period to many Cubans has translated as 'Miami's calling me'. It is perhaps the first time in modern history that Cuba can categorically consider itself truly 'independent'.

Cultural displacement wasn't an option for Ernesto. Soy Cubano (I am Cuban) was his message, but his strong proud tone changed to a whisper and his full eyes narrowed when provoked. This was going to be one of the many critical conversations I had entered, in what is principally a totalitarian state. Everything has to pass via El Comandante, who has the stealth of a cheetah and more lives than ordinary cats.

Ernesto took me to the Students' Union, which was a magnificent colonial mansion. He explained, 'Political activity is encouraged here, but strictly within the principal ideas of the Revolutionary Government. No other party exists outside of the Young Communists of Cuba. It's not advisable to speak publicly about ideas that go against the order. Of course, in the privacy of your own home, you can express your ideas as you wish. We, as Cubans, often debate and argue our political and economic situation with family and friends. We do not all agree. I, being younger, wish for greater freedom of speech and World integration. But we believe in Socialist principals. Every citizen of Cuba is considered equal and an integral part of our society. We value our heroes and our heroines, literature, vibrant history, schools, hospitals and, above all, the fact that we have independence. Without this, we will return to being a "semicolony", an Island of new slavery – none of us wish for that again. We are REBELS. You've seen the word painted on the street walls. Maybe it is time again. We need a new Revolution that involves youth, younger ideas and the vitality of a young and intellectual mind. You can't tell me that a country that celebrates its Revolutionary past with fervour will never have another Revolution in its history! Does it all stop with the triumph in 1959? No, Señor.

'The problem is more serious than ever because it is harder than ever to rise up from the underground with a united faction. Castro started his revolutionary activity in this very building as a student. He spoke out. Students and intellectuals listened to his rebellious ideas, ideas that inspired a union, a group of people that would later fight as an army, and then as a nation. He was audacious, projecting himself from the tops of public monuments so that his voice would carry. A carefree attitude is a mark of youth. With youth, you have everything to live for and everything to lose. He knows that the sword alone serves only to unleash immature aggression. Only through the intellect of the mind and pen can the sword be employed to full effect.

'But how hard it is for us to debate and write when freedom of speech isn't permitted in a university building, an establishment that throughout history has been the breeding ground for new ideas and leaders. Castro is aware that he formed his ideas within a university environment. He debated, printed leaflets and created an underground movement that went against the current. Taking this into account, he has been quick to introduce policies that have curbed student movements. Because of this, further Revolutionary ideas have been unable to fuse, although they are debated. The word "REBEL" refers to Castro's Cuba for the moment. In the eyes of the World we are radical, aren't we? Real Rebels. More than just rhetoric?'

I pondered on Ernesto's question. It was true, Cuba is radical. I never walk round my city and see Government publicity based on the meaning of the word 'Rebel'. The only thing we see that is pathetically used as a shock factor is sex, and that is low-key compared to what is going on today in Cuba. But how literally can you take this word 'Rebel'? I would argue that Cuba defines the meaning of the word. One important national holiday is known as 'the day of the heroic guerrilla'. I find it amazing that a country celebrates such a day – Che Guevara's day of remembrance. No Morris dancers performing here on May Day.

'Rebel' also means 'Real'. It's a history of real struggles involving recent heroes and heroines; the centuries of struggle continue. 'Real' because its struggle comes from within; 'Rebel' because it resists the exterior, the foreign that exploits the beleaguered.

Europeans sailed to adventure, discover, conquer, possess, dispossess, and gain prestige. But once they procured New Worlds, Europeans then had to defend what they had forcefully claimed. By contrast, Cuba has always had to fight to regain what was its in the first instance, namely, an independence that is not tied to neocolonial activity. It has, therefore, principally been an interior struggle that started with the Indian fighting the Spaniard and currently stops with the romantic rebel fighting the imperialist superpower.

Cuba takes a daring and unique stand in the World. At the conference of Latin American countries, Cuba stands alone as an independent country whose dreams still shine in the impassioned 'free' verses of its poet/hero/revolutionary icon José Martí and in that immortalized glare of determination in Che Guevara's eyes. 'Hasta la victoria siempre' (Always forward until victory) was the famous defining phrase. Cuba still to this very day inspires this – look at whose face is displayed on the banners every time the Latin American people take to the streets in order to protest.

'Rebel' because its speakers stand on the World platform at the United Nations and denounce imperialism, World poverty and exploitation. During the 1960s, the World looked on as Che Guevara and Castro took centre stage, dressed in combat gear, and spoke with passion, pointing their fingers and denouncing the imperialists' machinery. 'Rebels' because they were the men the World loved and the media focused on.

Castro is still bringing in huge crowds. On a recent trip to Jamaica, a BBC World Service reporter said:

The people remained transfixed as he spoke for over two hours. This is very uncommon in Jamaica where after half an hour the people normally require a break. On this day, however, the atmosphere was of excitement. Jamaica wishes to re-form ties with Cuba, saying that they were severed at a period when the government was influenced by US policy in the region.

'Real' because their struggles haven't been won by buying the favours of billionaire media tycoons. I couldn't list the number of programmes and book titles that I've seen predicting the Revolution's downfall. What these authors fail to grasp is that this is a struggle that comes from within the soul, from an almost tragic fairy-tale beginning. Cuba's history is stained with the blood of its people, who ironically were brought to the Island from the exterior, their enemy, and died fighting from the interior.

Cuba's history is far too evocative, too tragic, too passionate and too far-reaching to be ignored. A photo of Che, Camilo, Fidel and Raúl Castro, Augusto Martínez Sánchez, Juan Almeida and Ramiro Valdez captures the essence of this long history and brings it all into the present tense. You keep looking, keep thinking. The word 'Rebel' is painted on another street corner. It reads the same.

'Ernesto,' I said, 'One of the main objectives of the Revolution was to educate the people so they no longer had to look up to the man with Knowledge and Words. This has been achieved beyond many Western standards. I have spoken to a cross-section of Cuban society and nobody that I've met has been unable to offer a point of view. In Peru and Bolivia, I came across many people who couldn't read or write, many who had no concept of another continent, another time, another place. Cubans know about their country and the exterior World. Education has made this possible.'

Ernesto simply nodded. Yet in some ways, I figured that this superior level of education could also be a factor that may bring about the next revolution. Cubans now are generally aspiring to greater things. They have been educated out of a state of dependency and beyond the Revolution's physical and economic capabilities at present. People are thinking and desiring change now. But few are not grateful for what has been achieved. Perhaps, the pen in the long run has been mightier than the sword. The question is 'will the sword need to be employed again'? Heavy policing and lengthy bureaucracy may make change harder to achieve, but nothing remains the same indefinitely.

It was time to leave Havana. My work was finished and the road to Trinidad was beckoning. Jules was already there, filming and expecting me.

April 23rd

I arrived at Havana's railway station at 8 am, sweating in the morning sun and from the weight of my rucksack. I hadn't booked a ticket, but I knew that the train to Sancti Spíritus was due to leave at 9.20 am. From there I would have to negotiate a Wah Wah to Trinidad de Cuba, as it was no longer served by an operational train route. Outside the station, there was a heated commotion from all angles. I loved it. Spanish sounds different when spoken with urgency. Everybody was in a hurry and few appeared to be getting anywhere. Cubans take a long time to issue tickets. It involves identity papers and paperwork. As one person exited the ticket office, the ticket issuer would give the nod and another person would scramble in past the guards. Watching this commotion from a distance, I made up my mind that at all costs I would get on that train, ticket or no ticket. Soy extranjero, señor.

The queue was disorderly and somehow I got sucked into the agitation. We crashed against the security lady who straddled the doorway. 'This won't do,' I thought, 'I'll get into the station and get on the train. When the ticket inspector comes, I'll plead ignorance.' Unfortunately, the entrance to the platform was also guarded and a similar scene was unfolding. The security guard was checking each person's ticket against their identity papers. Only when all was correct could one pass onto the platform area. Strangely, I was enjoying the hustle and bustle, in spite of only having had three and a half hours' sleep.

The sweep of the queue eventually pushed me towards the guard. I pulled out a scrap of dirty white paper from my back pocket and he signalled me through. It was like stepping through a waterfall. All the abuse, invasion and roaring noise could be heard behind me. The tranquillity in front was more welcoming. The girl behind the information desk was yawning and manicuring her nails; she had peroxide-blonde hair, which looked very unnatural on a Cuban.

'The train to Sancti Spíritus?' I inquired.

'Cancelled,' she said. 'Accident on the line. Mañana hay otro.'

I hadn't time to take this in before she whistled to a companion. Another young woman appeared and led me through a side door. I found myself looking at the heaving crowd from inside the ticket office. We had entered via a back door that conveniently avoided the mayhem outside.

'We reimburse you.'

'No, no. I must travel today. Anywhere in a southerly direction from Havana, preferably near Trinidad. What are my options – go to Santa Clara first, then take a bus?'

'There is a train leaving at 1.30 this afternoon. It will drop you at a place called Guayos. From there you make your way to Trinidad.'

'Yes. I haven't bought a ticket yet. Sorry.'

She reached into her breast pocket and pulled out a ticket book, fumbling with the carbon copy while gazing at the madness. In Cuba, there must always be a copy of some sorts.

'Nine US dollars.'

'OK. Let me leave my rucksack in your office, please.'

I had four hours to pass, so I thought I'd check out the famous Hotel Inglaterra, write postcards and drink my first white coffee. The hotel terrace is admittedly a decorative place, where you can escape from the madness of Havana's streets while still looking and listening to everything on them. All prices are in dollars. I enjoyed my morning there very much.

The train left on time rocking on the tracks. An old revolutionary informed me that the track hadn't been used for many years and the driver was obliged to go slower as he wasn't sure whether the track was intact. This daunting prospect became a reality when the carriage would momentarily leave the track, dropping down to the next rail that had sunk several inches over the years. The journey was very slow. At the junction Two Kings, the train stopped while the driver's carriage was unhitched, transferred to another line and reconnected to what was the rear of the train. This was a perfect moment for the local inhabitants to boost their annual income. They hovered outside windows shouting out the names of the dishes that they had prepared. I thought about eating something. The choice was oranges, bananas, ham rolls or a serving of ham and rice. I was too slow in my decision-making. All was quickly sold. I prepared myself for another day of going hungry and sank into my book.

It wasn't long after the train started rolling backwards that a lad passed down the aisle selling food from a supermarket trolley. He had a cheeky vibe about him, which I reckoned was due to the fact that his cuisine was far from mouthwatering. However, it was OK for a starving adventurer whose trousers now hung from his hip bones, exposing stomach to private hairs. Twelve Cuban pesos bought me a cardboard carton of food - rice, beans and ham and five chocolate bars wrapped in silver foil. You'll eat pretty much anything when you're starving, including the Cuban equivalent of Spam and pork pie. Nothing for vegetarians, short of picking out the ham and munching on the rice and beans.

The train arrived in Santa Clara at midnight. By this time I felt bloated and windy, as did my neighbour, although he was less discreet about it. Santa Clara is where Che's remains now lie. During the Revolution, he derailed a loaded munitions train destined for Batista's tyrannical army. History reports it as being a 'heroic victory'. I wondered if the train of the 1950s had gone any faster than the current service. If not, this heroic derailment seems somewhat fantastical. Che Guevara and his column of troops would have been able to board the moving train by running after it!

I decided to stay on the train at Santa Clara, as it was now too late to catch a bus to Trinidad. My best option was to get off at Guayos, as the girl had told me in Havana, and wait in the station till morning. From there I would be able to catch the first Wah Wah to Sancti Spiritus where the transport to Trinidad was more reliable.

On the roadside in Guayos by the Wah Wah stop, there was a large collection of campesinos (Cuban farmers). They all appeared to respect some sort of cultural code made apparent in their sombreros, their mannerisms and the smoking of home-rolled cigars. All of them had wrinkled brown oily faces like walnuts that had been cracked open, doused in oil and left to perish in the sun. They also had sacks, what my grandmother calls 'bit bags', by their sides like faithful pets. I sat down and bid them all buenas días.

A chorus of buenas días echoed back. I was rapidly offered a 'tabaco, muy bueno' which was slotted in the corner of my mouth with practised art. Another campesino put the fire to the stick and, before I knew it, I was one of the boys. I had to show a brave face smoking such a strong cigar at four in the morning, having had no sleep and a desperate scrap of a meal. Yet, somehow, I felt welcomed into this country entourage. I almost looked the part in jeans and a shirt, plenty of facial stubble, a cigar's full sizzling disc burning away in the blackness, and a bag by my side. But I wore no sombrero, I sported no moustache and I didn't have an oily walnut face.

A campesino led me to a street stall round the corner. I could smell Cuban coffee and an oil lamp in the morning air. The coffee was cheap, so cheap that I bought everyone a cup without realizing that I'd spent any money. The coffee was served thick, sugary and in small amounts. As we all sat drinking with our feet on the dusty road, various conversations sprang up. I asked them what they were all doing in such a desolate place at four in the morning. This struck me as being a perfectly reasonable question. I obviously had no choice in the matter, circumstances having determined that I should be one of the first to witness the day taking shape. To the campesinos, however, this was a nonsensical question. One of them replied, 'We're here at this early hour every day to go to the fields. Oh, except Sunday – the wife's day. We spend all Sunday at la casa dedicating her lots of flattery.'

At this recollection lots of gruff grunts grunted forth in agreement, 'Si, si.'

'La casa [house].'

'La mujer [wife].'

'Asi, es la vida [Such is life].'

I changed the angle. 'So, what time is the Wah Wah coming?'

'Oh soon, you'll see.'

'Yes, but do you know an approximate time?' I said, trying to clear up the vagueness.

'Five-thirty, six o' clock.'

'What? So why have you all come here so early? You could have stayed in bed for a few hours longer.'

'Hombre, we always meet at this time. We enjoy a smoke, greet one another, drink some coffee. You see, this is how we are. This is how we do things.'

Another chorus of buenas días grunted from all those present, and then an elderly gentleman joined the gathering. He was well dressed, though his trousers fell about five inches short of his ankles. He had that look of old Spanish-Cuban landed gentry. He'd obviously been a looker in his day, the type that liked to shake peach trees and catch the falling ripe fruit. He addressed me and immediately I recognized a cheerful character. I learned that he'd also been on the train from Havana. He was now a priest in Old Havana. My first words to him were a mark of courtesy. Something simple like, 'Long journey, hey, señor'?

He replied, as if he was picking up on a question that he would have preferred me to ask him, 'I'm 82 years old. At 57, I found the tranquillity of Christ. The Bible has raised many good issues, good morals. No, no, no, señor. I'm more tranquilo now. Thanks be to God.'

'Oh no,' I thought, 'a bible lesson at this godforsaken hour!' Though it is true that the Bible does contain some marvellous literature.

'Myself, I prefer Don Quixote,' I said reflecting on the knight's eccentricities, his morals, faith and the good nature in which he practised all of them. It was a hell of an hour to start debating religion or Señor Quixote's morals in comparison to the Bible's. We needed to change the subject fast.

My priest campañero started up again, 'Before I reached 57, phew, I was an active old boy. At 55, I married my third wife. I've got lots of children – some in Havana, some abroad. When I was just 16, I met an older divorced lady who had a child. She was my professor of love. She took me by the reins and taught me everything I know.'

He nudged me and burst into laughter. His laugh contained all the naughtiness that he'd formerly had. Our priest was a jovial little man who, even at his age and after a hellish journey, was still full of beans. A campesino by his side asked him about God; the priest started to talk and all ears fell on the voice of authority. The only breaks in the silence were the crackles of drawn cigars and grunted responses to what the priest had to say. This reminded me of the scene with the man with knowledge spreading it among the crowds, which I've seen depicted in hundreds of 16th and 17th century paintings throughout Latin America.

The campesinos listened attentively to what the priest had to say. He answered their questions with confidence and candour. As the doors to my Wah Wah closed, I realized why they get up before dawn and share an early-morning moment together.

It was only when I arrived in Trinidad and recounted my sleepless night to Jules that I became aware of how bizarre the whole journey had been. But it also showed Cuba at its best and demonstrated that Cubans are sociable, they share what they've got and their friendship extends to everyone.

The railway station brings the World to this small town of Guayos. This is the beauty of the iron road.

April 24th – Trinidad

Described as a 'colonial jewel' and dedicated as such by UNESCO, Trinidad is indeed a jewel in a dull-gold setting. Dull gold is worth more on the World market, but it isn't to everyone's taste. Trinidad is just as the postcards show it, full of colonial atmosphere, at certain times only; at others, it appears more like the Golden Mile in Marbella, Andalucía. These quaint streets were built on the typical Spanish grid plan. The street activity is lazy until approximately ten o' clock, when spanking new tourist buses deliver the masses. Tourists step off the buses, divide into groups and walk off for two or three hours. Hastily, the locals carry signposts onto the streets with English and German translations of goods for sale. Suddenly, Trinidad isn't sleeping after all. Signposts read:

Tapes, Compact Discs for Sale

Cigars, Rum – all Brands Stocked

Traditional Folkloric Group – as Featured on TV

Music overtakes the morning calm. Men playing dominoes in the shade quickly exchange their hands for double basses and tres guitars. The tourists extend their zoom lenses, snap away happily and buy cassette tapes of recorded music for $5 each. This goes on until about four in the afternoon, when the buses depart. The signposts are then hidden from state do-gooders and the television sets are switched on, LOUD. They have a right to make a living and this is how a proportion of Trinidad's population does it.

I wasn't enthralled by Trinidad, in spite of it being a beautiful city with a lavish colonial history. I think its best offerings are architecture, geographical location, lovely cheap fish dinners served in private family homes, an abandoned railroad that winds solitarily up towards Spaghetti Western mountains and a maestro of the congas called Alberto. There was also an exciting period in Trinidad's history, when it was a haven for pirates. You can have a lot of fun cycling the ten or so kilometres to the Ancóna beach.

I had my first ugly moment in Trinidad. At night, most people watch soap operas on TV. You can hear them blaring into the streets, cutting through the evening's stillness. You can walk for many blocks and not see a soul, and then you see a light through a half-open door, with a sign above saying 'El Bar'. When we entered conversation ceased and the people stared at us. We were from out of town and outside visiting hours. A young tattooed Cuban came over and insisted on buying us beers. His T-shirt was riddled with holes, and he had an overall look that seemed to advise caution. He had a 'mullet' hairdo that is more associated with village Heavy Rock dudes – long at the back and cropped at the sides. I knew that it was best not to accept but, at the same time, declining would aggravate the situation. I felt pickled. His eyes were intense.

'No, gracias,' I said.

'I want buy you a beer. You accept. You think I don't have dollar. I have dollar and I buy. You think Cubans don't have dollar?'

I had wondered whether Cubans ever begrudge tourists for their wealth. This lad evidently resented us, not for who we were, but for what we were. Certainly the youth in tourist areas do harbour a bit of resentment, just as many older Cubans resent the economic necessity that has pushed many young Cuban girls into becoming jineteras. It must be made clear that jineteras live better than most Cubans do – for the moment.

Mixed with this historical air, Trinidad has an odour of both stale and fresh money. It has probably always been this way since the arrival of the landed gentry, who, in turn, lured the buccaneers and freebooters. The streets are pleasant, many cobbled and lined with telegraph wires, and the houses have spacious open-plan designs. The façades are interrupted by grand windows with wooden shutters which, when opened, allow you to peer into an ancient World. The internal patio is the heart of the house and all the rooms extend from it. The colours are Latin pastel shades of yellow, red, blue, brown and green. The town is built on a slight incline. From the top of the town you get a beautiful view of lacquered rooftops blurred by a hazy heat undulating from the sea.

In Trinidad, I rode my first bicycle the twelve kilometres to the sea. Mine was a Communist-manufactured bicycle, the Flying Pigeon. It really was like a flying pigeon, being clumsy, bulky, heavy, and ugly; yet it had a charm about it and was mountains of good fun. The seat was sprung like a Cuban bed. I bounced over every pothole as if I was making my way on a rusty pogo stick. The Flying Pigeon has a story. Castro imported millions of them from China when he announced the Special Period, thus alleviating transport problems to a certain degree, fuel being in short supply. People need a means of mobility and distributing bicycles was the Special Period's answer.

The Cubans have customized these bicycles. Consequently, they have boosted the Flying Pigeon's status to that of a 'Passable Parrot'. To the foreigner from the West, it is blissfully romantic to watch lovers or a family passing by, all sitting chatting on a single bicycle. One child often sits on a seat fixed onto the handlebars, another on the crossframe, while the mother sits side-saddle on a padded rack mounted over the back wheel. Of course, if any of them were given the choice between the bicycle and the car, it would be obvious what a Cuban family would prefer. However, this choice isn't on offer to all, so the Cubans continue to pedal along the streets ringing their bicycle bells at friends and pedestrians who block the road.

The Ancóna beach is well worth the ride. It is a long stretch of white sand swept by a turquoise sea. After a day's swimming, we started the uphill ascent to Trinidad, whose lights could be seen in the slopes of the mountain. On this road, I saw a big signpost. It didn't read 'Rebel', but carried a social message that occupied my thoughts all the way home:

In the world there are 200 million children sleeping in the streets
Not one of them is Cuban

I reflected on my travels throughout the Americas, Europe, Japan and the Indian subcontinent. I'd seen a great number of children sleeping in the streets. In India, railway-station platforms are home to whole families. Why? Because they have huge industrial-sized taps where people can wash and drink. They are also policed, so that families can sleep in relative security without being battered.

Somewhere in India, I arrived at the station just before sunrise. The floor was covered with sleeping bodies. I spotted a vacant space to sit down and carefully made my way over there. It reminded me of making my way to a stage at the Glastonbury Festival. I placed my rucksack down, sat on it, and waited for the train to pull up. A cow wandered onto the platform and started to piss – a long, steady, heavy piss. It was enjoying the sacred status that had been bestowed upon it. The piss bounced off the floor and sent spots onto the faces and bodies of the people in close proximity and then made its way across the station floor's imperfections before pooling against some unfortunate being.

It was pitiful to watch and yet, emerging from such ugliness was an act of beauty. The beauty of kindness always appears greatly intensified when coming from a person who is living on the threshold of poverty. The father of a sleeping family stirred, rubbed his eyes and blinked rapidly while trying to focus on me. He then woke his wife and three children, who all stared at me with their huge dark eyes while rolling up their bedding and amassing their belongings with a practised art.

The mother and two daughters went over to the tap and began washing their beautiful long black shiny hair. The father disappeared round the station corner and returned holding a throwaway ceramic cup at me. He was offering me a cup of tea. It was a gesture of humanity that crossed all boundaries of class, nationality and social status. It was also a simple offering from the hands of India's poorest and meant with the best intentions. Even though I don't take sugar, this was the best cup of tea that I'd ever had.

The sign read true. I had never seen a Cuban sleeping on the streets. In this aspect, Cuba is more intolerant of homelessness than the West. My city, Bristol, has homeless people hunched up and begging every 100 metres in the city centre.

On the road into Trinidad, we crossed a disused narrow-gauge railway line just to the south of the town. The track curved round to the left and then was lost in the looming awe of the mountains. It would have made a great photo entitled Solitude, or something cheesy in that vein. This was also a perfect location to shoot some clichéd 16 mm footage.

The following day we returned at the crack of dawn with the cameras. Jules was on it, eye to the lens, directing me around with a cigar wedged in the corner of his mouth.

La Cascada – The Waterfall of Enchantment

The pounding of the conga drums punished my ears, distorting my perception of the exotic jungle vegetation around me. A Walkman was enhancing my reality. The heavyweight wooden ring of the drums and the jungle surrounds made me feel like an adventurer from Spain's Golden Century, El Siglo de Oro. I'd recorded this persuasive percussion the previous night on my portable DAT player at a Santería-inspired backyard event. It was a timeless and weird event: sluggish bare feet pounded the dry earth to the magnifying power of the percussion maestro. It was hypnotic; twirling bodies stirred up the dust and the vision became sepia. In the centre was a black spiritualist who chanted a repetitive line. His voice was weighty and obscured amid the conga's bass frequencies. Other people replied to his chants in concert, but I became lost in a daze of dust that rose and fell like a tired-out lava lamp. My face was sprayed with rum. Someone spat it out in a fine spray that sweetened my face and partially woke me. This was Afro-Cuban Brujería, or witchcraft. I'd felt this organic state of reverie twice before in my life, once in India at the fortress/palace Chittaurgarh, which is a magical place. The other time was with Spanish gypsies in Andalucía.

At Chittaurgarh, when facing defeat in the hands of their enemies, the citizens practised a bizarre code of chivalry that demanded honour in death. By not submitting, they left nothing of themselves and victory was denied to the enemy. This may hold the key to the origins of Victory Tower that dominates the heart of Chittaurgarh. There is also a sacred pool.

My first moment of magic happened while I was at the pool's edge, having descended the carved stone steps that led to the pool. The passage was lit. Orange candles strongly perfumed the air. I stood ankle-deep in the pool and felt my feet tickled by the bodies of fish that brushed past me.

It was at this pool that a peerless Rajput Rani dedicated a part of her day, seated on a floating throne. This wasn't some obsession of hers, rather a duty. Her subjects, enchanted by her beauty, were not permitted by some social code to gaze directly at her. To overcome the problem, the beautiful Rani would spend a little narcissistic moment seated on her floating throne. Concealed within this throne, her reflection would be clearly visible upon the water's surface. In this manner, her beauty was indirectly admired. It was enough to satisfy her people, but not the lustful nature of conquering miscreants who terrorized the region and made her the object of their desires. The tale must remain incomplete, as the rarest and most delectable pleasures are those that are hinted at and never fully told. You can always seek out her reflection for yourself.

The tragedy is that hundreds of thousands of Chittaurgarh citizens died during the three sackings that this idyllic fort underwent during its magical existence – and all because of denied love. As I stood in the water, I observed the advancing moon. She had just begun to rise in a dusty vacuum. The atmosphere was compelling and strangely eerie; dusk is an instance of unveiling. At that moment, a warm breeze whipped across this sacred water catchment, blowing my hair back and sending shivers down my spine. The candles were extinguished and the smoke blackened the air, contaminating the scent and changing it into an odour of burnt life. Gusts of air resonated in my ears. I heard voices and the gallant cries of the hundreds of thousands of warriors who had died at the sword of the enemy, and of the women and children who had burned themselves on the pyre. Death rang momentarily in my ears. My body froze. It wasn't sheer terror I felt but a melange of tumultuous fear, curiosity and sadness. A deep sadness, as the cries of burning women and children echoed all around and penetrated me. My eyes ached from the black smoke and began to water. I turned but I couldn't see the steps to take me away from this darkened scene. I'm glad that I stayed and lingered at the sacred pool's edge where death hinted at a mysterious presence and the moon silently bore witness to it all; together we heard the cries of past times.

The second moment of magic occurred in Andalucía, Spain, on Christmas Eve 1995. I was in the Sacromonte neighbourhood of Granada. The evening air was still. From time to time, a church bell chimed and broke the calm. I remember that I wasn't looking for anything in particular, just in a curious frame of mind and ready to go with the night.

Sacromonte is constructed on the opposite hillside to the Alhambra palace/fortress. The Arabic turrets and reddish brick walls pierce through the obscurity cast down upon them from the looming Sierra. The Alhambra was built by Nasrid Sultan Princes. They built it with layers upon layers of secret intricacies - inspired by love. They were silent poets who strummed their lutes in gardens fed by trickling cool waters. All around, arches beckon you to enter into this once-Moorish illustrious wonder in Southern Spain.

The guitar instrumental 'Recuerdos de la Alhambra', written by Tárrega, tells all you need to know about this poetically composed World. The guitar melody wafts you hypnotically around the secret passageways that open out onto delightful gardens surrounded by perfectly constructed archways. It's peerless, and has been the source of creation for many of Spain's greatest musicians, such as Manuel de Falla and Andrés Segovia.

Sacromonte holds the key to a very different existence. It's a neighbourhood that has always been a dwelling for Spain's gypsies, who originated from as far away as Old India. It is a barrio that is also lost in history, but much less romantically so, because Sacromonte still carries its gypsy tomfoolery right up to the present day. Once the women toiled and conned passers-by in order to make a living, as did the men. The Moorish Princes – the Nasrid Sultans, lived in the confines of a majestic fairy-tale World, whereas the gypsies opposite lived in caves carved into the hillside rock. They scraped a rude existence out of Andalucía's red tierra that the Moors so worshipped in prayer and verse.

Today, the caves have whitewashed interiors. They have also been extended outwards by building façades that resemble ordinary houses. Gypsies still live here, but without the hustle and bustle of the old gypsy life. Gone are the activities from the streets: women washing; men building; everyone trading, bartering, gossiping, out in the fields or in the town selling; children playing; animals wandering in and out of caves; horses jogging with carts to the command of the gypsy. Now, Sacromonte enjoys the tranquillity that the Andalucían sun casts over the afternoon.

One evening I was sitting on a wall looking across at the Alhambra, thinking how Andalucía had been the land of 'red earth', or known by the Moors as 'Al-andalus'. It was the colour that had so captured the hearts and fancies of the Moorish adventurers, scholars and nobility. The peace was such that I failed to hear about 20 people approaching until they were upon me. The men were all dressed in black suits with waistcoats and white shirts. The women were in colourful swirling trajes flamencos, (flamenco dresses). Everyone talked and walked in an excited manner, except an older man who lagged behind the group. He stopped to salute me and ask what I was doing sitting there. I told him that I had been listening out for the 'Moor's last sigh', El

Suspiro del Moro. This seemed to please him enormously and he laughed, tapping my shoulder.

Of course, it sounds fantastic, but it is true that on January 2nd 1492 the final ruling Sultan, Boabdil, shut the doors of his inherited fairy-tale kingdom behind him for the very last time and sought refuge in the Sierra. He was escaping the onslaught of Catholicism and its marching army. Later, from a safe vantage point, the retreating Boabdil turned towards his beloved Alhambra and watched the Spanish troops take control. The Sultan was rumoured to have dropped to his knees and said a prayer to Allah before sighing a million sighs for the treasure that he had lost. His majestic World, built by the poet's subdued hand and musing mind over many centuries, was now a series of memories best left where they first began – in a verse and a song.

My gypsy friend called out to the rest of the group. They stopped, turned and faced us. He said, 'I want you to meet Tomatito. He's just given a concert in the theatre and now we're going to a cave, to a friend of the family. We play flamenco, dance and drink.'

Tomatito swept his guitar case further round his shoulder and extended his hand. I shook hands with Spain's number one flamenco guitarist – just like that. Tomatito is the young star who accompanied and made up an integral part of the flamenco legend Camarón de la Isla. Camarón became a gypsy legend after he reached huge popular acclaim across Spain and died young of AIDS, caused by drug abuse.

'Vamos,' signalled Tomatito waving his arms forward and the band of gypsies and I paced on. We stopped outside a cave's entrance and a lad went in to make some inquiries. Shortly after, the lights were on and we were all inside. A quickly assembled bar was rapidly decorated with beers, spirits and wines. Jackets were hung up all over the place and Tomatito began playing 'Bulerías' with vigour. He was seated in the centre of the cave's deepest point, and his friends strummed an accompaniment to his lead.

The night progressed, the music got louder, the singing more intense, and the dancing firmer. Suddenly I became aware that I was absorbing a tradition as old as the Iberian Peninsula itself – the gypsy and his guitar. An audacious-looking girl caught my eye. She sat, composed and silent in a corner, but the profundity of her dark eyes hid many lies. Without warning, she rose and poised, ready to dance. She started with twirling movements of her arms and then extended her fingers. Her hips rolled while her feet hammered the floor. The noise escalated as she clapped her hands rigorously in a complex rhythm.

Tomatito followed her rhythm. She forced him to play faster until he was slapping his fingertips across all the strings and guitar body. His head was bowed over the guitar in full concentration. Her hair swept through the air, covering her in fine black magic. Her thighs vibrated as if in orgasm.

Her soul was hovering as if trapped in the charged cellar air. It was instructing her to go beyond her physical limits. She stretched, threw her head backwards and arched her arms upwards and outwards as if following the contours of a comet. 'Uno, dos, tres,' went the shouts. She pulled herself upright, brought forward a single arm and froze. Her hair dropped down, half covering her eyes. Tomatito looked up, sweat pouring down his temple. 'Olé!' screamed the gypsy fraternity.

She started again. Her hand movements were very complex and impossible to focus sharply on. I could see her, followed by her ghostly naked soul, all blurring into separate entities of the same person. She froze again, rigid, sweating as if nailed to a post. Her eyes pierced mine but she wasn't looking at me. She was in a trance. I suddenly realized that I was perched on the edge of the bench by a hair's breadth. Sweat was running from under my hair and the salt was stinging my eyes.

I hardly spoke for three days after that night with Spain's

flamenco gypsies.

Back in Cuba

As I started the descent to the waterfall, I was still somewhat overcome by the previous night's Afro-Cuban black magic. The conga rhythm in my headphones was revitalizing vivid images. The jungle path tapered into a thin rocky track, overgrown on both sides by tropical vegetation. Huge palm trees rustled their knife-like leaves in the afternoon breeze. Birds shrieked loudly in a repetitive monotone that filtered through my headphones, accompanying the conga drums. Their calls were new and evocative sounds to my ears. I never saw the birds but I would occasionally spot a gliding shadow moving over the jungle floor and crossing my path.

I was a long way from where Columbus is said to have landed, although this was a stopping-off point for Cortez before he set sail for Mayan Mexico. I wondered whether he'd found a similar trail, and what his impressions might have been. Unlike Cortez, I'd seen such Caribbean thick vegetation in books and films and on television. However, it's very different actually being there, and alone. I am an explorer and adventurer and this was a camino, a path that evoked many thoughts and stimulated all the senses. I was alert, excited and determined.

Darting from rock to rock wasn't a problem; I'd had a youth's zest for the mountains in North and South America, on the fells in the Lake District, England and in the Scottish Highlands. There were an abundance of trees and roots to hang onto, if need be. I tried to pace myself in half time to the congas but it became an impossible task. I tripped on a rock and slipped, stirring up dry dusty earth as I fell. I dropped to a rock ledge and grabbed a protruding root with precision. A lizard stared cockily at me from the underside of a rock wall, his tongue tasting the dust. He scuttled daintily along with nimble toes. I followed him with my eyes while hanging onto the tree root and realized that the path was now leading under a rock overhang.

My headphones had slipped from my ears in the tumble. I pulled myself up and heard a distant cooing sound echo through the jungle. I was having doubts about my orientation skills, when I heard a faint sound of cascading water. There wasn't far to go. I pulled myself up and set off with a rapid step. Sweat was causing my clothes to sag off me and lose shape. The noise of water grew louder until I glimpsed a sparkle from off the water's surface. Through the dark green fleshy-veined leaves I could see a pool of light aqua shades. As I rounded the final bend, I saw the liquid crystal dropping from a V-shaped overhang of rock. The sun was positioned directly between the V. The strong rays highlighted rainbow colours in the crystal splinters of the water. This was paradise in an exotic jungle setting. It was as exciting for me approaching the 21st century as it must have been for the first European explorers who, having never known such nature, drew pictures and wrote notes to show the people back home how this New World was made up.

From atop a rock ledge I peered into the depths of the pool. I could see shadows below the surface. The movement was a bizarre scuttling. I tore my clothes off and stood ready to dive into another dream. The water was clean and fresh. I came to the surface and called out. My voice echoed off the vertical walls and birds rapidly took off in fright. I suddenly found myself in complete solitude. Looking upwards, I could see thin hanging vines rising to infinity. Maybe this wasn't real. Maybe I was enchanted like Don Quixote had been when he descended into Montosino's Cave. But the experience hadn't been that fortunate for him, although it had been enlightening. After several days lost in obscure thought within the cave, Don Quixote finally emerged, but shortly thereafter he withered and died. Why? What had changed his vision while reflecting in the depths of the Earth's obscurity?

He found the reality of a World he considered insane. A World that, in turn considered him insane. His eccentricities were misconstrued as madness and his perfect vision of a wonderful World was deemed unreal. He was finally defeated by modernity, by progress, by the simple truth that the World cannot be contained in a book. Society is for ever charging full steam ahead without much regard for the past, as he did while tilting at windmills. Today, Don Quixote's imagination still testifies that the way forward is to look to the past and carry the good from it with you into the future.

Could Revolutionary Cuba learn a thing or two from Don Quixote? Cervantes' ingenious novel had certainly been the inspiration for Simón Bolívar, the liberator of Latin America, and for Che Guevara. Maybe Cuba's leaders should descend into the depths of the Earth and think about their visions. Mine were showing smallish cracks and imperfections. Cuba is no longer a country of romantic rebellion, although the struggle continues with fervour and jaded passion; it is a country governed by leaders whose visions are perhaps too ideal and steadfast. It's on a path that will never lead to a waterfall of enchantment, and yet the water flows cleaner than anywhere that I've been to.

'Patria o muerte [Homeland or Death]' insist the slogans on the walls. I fear this current vision can only improve when the path leads to another predetermined destiny. New ideas are needed.

Forgive me, my beloved Cuba, for being so frank, I am on your side. But I hear your people speak of greater World integration and change. New visions and ideas must evolve. This isn't to say that the people to whom I have spoken are not proud of what their current Revolution has achieved. Cubans possess an overwhelming unity of spirit. This unity has been attained through a common belief that every Cuban has had to make sacrifices along the bumpy road towards sovereignty. For those Cubans in Miami, who may be rubbing their hands in glee at the thought of cracks appearing, let me quickly add that this change, they say, should not be dictated by neo-imperialist US policy, from which practically the whole of Central and Latin America has suffered. Cubans are looking to other markets; opening up trade with Latin America, Canada and, inevitably, Europe. Slowly they are embracing Capitalist markets whereby trade is undertaken based upon 'mutual respect' and 'manageable time scale'.

The following quotation that appeared in The Guardian Newspaper on January 11th 1999, written by Jonathan Glancey, goes much of the way to expressing this same view:

'We have to sit back and watch while developers from Spain, Mexico and elsewhere in the Americas move in to Havana... We could be doing hotels in the city, resorts outside... All this anti-Castro shit is just a waste of everyone's time,' said one small-time Miami developer with big plans for the future of Havana. The Miami-Cuban invasion of Havana is talked about over cold beers and improbable rum cocktails in pistachio-green bars and icing-sugar-pink cafés, but because property investment by US citizens in Cuba is illegal, the players in the wings keep mum despite the rum. The Castro regime can be criticized for any number of reasons, yet Cuba itself, and Havana above all, is making friends and influencing investment decisions worldwide. Meanwhile, the 6000 delegates who attended last year's Free Trade Association of the Americas (FTAA) at Belo Horizonte voted overwhelmingly in favour of including Cuba in their ranks.

He went even further in his article:

Forget the military. The real threat to Cuba's gloriously ravaged colonial capital is invasion by property developers who want to turn it into a candy-coloured mall.

US property development, foreign policy and external dictatorship are, therefore, considered offensive. As Castro himself said, when talking about the Special Period, 'It is undeniably tough, we endure a cruel economic blockade, but have we not redistributed land to the workers, achieved racial equality, surpassed our expectations of health and education, shared a generosity of wealth throughout a beautiful and historic Pueblo? For the first time in our New History we can truly say "We Are Independent." To lose all of these Revolutionary principles would be a return to our pitiful condition before 1959. It would be a return to new forms of slavery. History would repeat. Do we really want this?'

I gazed below the surface while treading water and again saw shadows. There was something big down there, and in abundance. The air was suddenly still. A cloud blocked the sun and the pool darkened. I was shivering and wanted to get out. The enchantment was over. I swam to the far end of the pool, where the current picked up and the water ran away into a river. I was perched on a rock, staring into space when my attention was caught again by that same movement. I was looking at a massive freshwater lobster; then I spotted another and another. I'd never seen such big lobsters in fresh water. They are supposed to be delicious when grilled with garlic. Their pincers were like hammerheads, and menacing: my return was overdue. I started the long ascent.

April 27th–May 3rd

It was a long overnight journey on the train to Santiago. Fortunately, I had been advised on a cheap and cheerful place to stay that was located in Calle Corona, one block down from the Central Park. I was soon settled, unpacked and on the streets again. Santiago rises steadily upwards from the port. The temperature was several degrees higher than in Havana. The narrow colonial streets are stuffy but have plenty of character. Telephone wires weave overhead, as do electric cables that power 1950s neon shop signs. It reminded me of one-time San Francisco, USA.

After a week discovering Santiago and its environs, I came to realize that not much happens during the working week with regard to nightlife. Fridays and Saturdays are when the city comes to life. The time to visit is during the street carnival; then it must surely be electric. Santiago is no more of a rival city to Havana than Birmingham is to London, but Santiago's baseball team certainly rivals Havana's. I explored the city, striving to avoid the heat. The barrio that had the most life was also rumoured to be the most dangerous - Chincharrones. It reminded me of a Barrio Latino, a kind of Hip-hop Barrio.

For the Cubans who do not live there, it is deemed a pit of low morality. However, I could always hear the laughter of the children echoing round me while they played street games. It appeared a hive of activity and movement. The houses were very old and emanated a decaying grace. I loved it.

I was invited into the house of a young girl called Yilean. She was lively, always smiling and sprightly. Her father offered me coffee and a seat on their rickety sofa. The springs were taut and charged and there were no cushions to ease the experience. I sipped the thick brown earthy coffee with tears in my eyes. Their house was very small, unpainted and darkly grey. It resembled a garage and had the same feel and smell (her father and brother were both mechanics). 'Grim' is the adjective that comes to mind.

Her father went behind a curtain doorway and returned with a Monte Cristo cigar. He had chosen the perfect hour for us to while away in each other's company. A perfect heat to escape while puffing on a Habano and drinking sweet coffee.

We talked about education. Yilean was extremely bright, and the great hope of the impoverished family. You got the impression that she was the flower that he'd decided to tend and lend his full attention to, as if he'd chanced upon her one fine morning pushing upwards from a pile of construction rubble. She was obviously her Dad's pride and joy, for he looked at her with unwavering affection. The father was a character; his white skin shone like a lighthouse when surrounded by his brown family. Santería beads bunched round his neck and fell loosely onto a loose belly. His eyes were magnified tenfold by his plastic-rimmed glasses. He could have been the unknown member of Run DMC.

He really did have a lot to rap about, supporting a large family at the lowest social level. The house had no proper lighting; electric wires protruded from the plaster finish waiting for the purchase of fixtures and fittings. There were no services connected for running water and his gas stove was a two-ring affair that resembled a well-used and beat-up camping model. The kitchen wall was charred from gas fumes. The house badly needed painting; I made up my mind to buy some white paint and freshen it up. On the way to the backyard dealer – ordinary Cubans never go to a state shop when the black market can provide them with the same but cheaper – Yilean told me that her father often drowned his sorrows with barrio rum.

'He's a good strong man despite everything,' she said.

Yilean was a resourceful girl and she had a grand vision of the World but, like most Cubans, she would have to fight all the way simply to break free from her barrio life. Alternately, the World may come to her – she has the charm, the sweetness and the intelligence to achieve her own goals.

I felt a sense of satisfaction from having brought some bright sunshine into their family home. The difference made by white emulsion on the walls is astonishing. When the job was done, we sipped coffee and puffed like wise seers after a good deed on the endless supply of Monte Cristo cigars that appeared from behind the curtained-off room. The father sat back in his chair, content with the brilliant walls. The smoke slowly rose and began to flavour the paint as it was drying.

I bade the family farewell, promising to write and send books to Yilean. The encounter with Yilean's family in Chincharrones has confirmed a few beliefs, namely, that many Cubans of the barrio do live in poverty and that good people exist there, just as anywhere. Yilean's father was an honest hard-working mechanic with a genuine love for his family and their interests.

Cuba, like any country, has a class structure. The outskirts often remain out of sight and out of mind.

There are always those who have and those who won't ever have. I still wish to believe in Che promoting a workforce that built an independent country of equality – the leader working with the proletariat. This simply was not the case. In central Old Santiago, conditions were far superior to those in the barrios. The houses in the central zones met with European standards. Yilean's barrio needed a lot of investment and work in order to meet these modern basic requirements.

May 1st is the 'Day of the Worker'. It is a national holiday and a fiesta of sorts. It's also a show of solidarity and pride for the Cuban worker. Yilean's father is a role model for the type of Cuban this day is dedicated to. It's the way in which the Revolution thanks the workforce for their faith, loyalty and efforts. The workers amassed very early in the morning. By 7 am the streets around Calle 4 were packed with rowdy, rum-swilling jovial faces. Everyone was in high spirits, singing and shouting aloud.

I saw banners of Che held aloft, others with the words

'Viva El Primer Día Del Mayo'. Music was, as ever, prominent. People chanted in concert; some let loose, vibrating their hips and shoulders in carnival mood. Faces and dark eyes momentarily glanced at me, bloodshot with barrio rum that could have fired a self-assembly rocket to Venus. A hand nudged me with what appeared to be a bottle of seven-year-old Havana Club and I swigged liberally. I was pushed along, moving with the crowd. Rattles added menace to the raucous. I couldn't spot the percussionists although I could hear them close by. We kept swigging as Plaza Martí came into the picture.

In the plaza the crowd movement swirled and collected like a river that runs into a dam. We listened to speakers. The heat was intense, tapping my crown like a shipbuilder nailing home a rivet into sheet metal. I felt relieved when the dam burst and we started gushing into one of the major streets that led to Santiago's centre. The bottle was in my hand again. The neat rum was as comfortable round my lips as alcohol pads are on open wounds. The chanting was now becoming less defined. The procession was losing people. They were breaking off, heading towards side streets, houses, parks and shop doorways. I got the feeling that events on the streets were coming to an end. The midday heat had defeated everyone. Now was the time for lunch, siesta and rest at home until the evening when it all started afresh.

My day, however, was just beginning, and now was the chance to visit the Santa Ifigenia cemetery. Castro himself comes here twice a year for spiritual guidance by visiting the tomb of José Martí, Cuba's most celebrated poet and leader of armed independence struggle against Spanish colonial rule.

The Virgin 1608

An open-backed lorry will take you out of Santiago towards the lush mountains and the peaceful village of El Cobre. When you jump off there, you'll find men selling candles, prayer pamphlets and flowers. You must buy these inexpensive little offerings for the Virgin. She is a legend and she stands proud, being Cuba's 'Patroness of Humanity'. Her status is such that she is the most revered icon of Cuban Catholicism, as well as being the goddess of Love in Santería. Her mythical status arose from a poignant yet charming fairy-tale beginning.

The Virgin was taken aboard a Spanish galleon in Santiago as booty. Maybe one of the sailors or merchants returning to Europe had taken a fancy to her and felt it within his right to remove her from her abode. However, it wasn't to be. For some inexplicable reason, she never made the transatlantic journey. She was tossed overboard and left to ride the sea as an abandoned, stolen and unwanted mannequin. It was two women slaves looking out across the Bay of Santiago who spotted her.

It is rumoured that she cried out to the slaves, who swore blindly that they felt a magic aura all round her. She radiated a soothing purple light as she was washed ashore. Their own arrival on these shores, in such hostile and uncaring conditions, drew instant parallels. Hence, their love for her was immediate and would undoubtedly have been enhanced by a label that was attached to her with the words:

Soy la Virgin de la Caridad

A 'Virgin of Charity' was just what these two slaves needed: they were destitute. The magic of life had been drained from their very souls. When it all appeared to be over, as if sent by a miracle, the Virgin was floating on the waves towards them in answer to their

prayers. The two slaves plucked her lovingly out of the water and read the label out aloud. This was how she was named.

It was some years afterwards that the Virgin was placed in a church and dressed up in fine attire so that other impoverished people could come and speak to her. The Virgin's reputation spread rapidly as people confirmed her willingness to help, love and console the needy. Cuba was the ideal home for such a charitable goddess as the people were perishing from the oppression of slavery, colonial rule and violent insurrections. I strolled up the street towards the church that houses her, knowing that Pope John Paul II had made exactly the same pilgrimage a month earlier.

The church is a pretty yellow with Latin red decorations. It stands forlorn, colourful and somewhat nostalgic, against a backdrop of mountains and distant copper mines. All around, one can hear the sounds of heat – the cracking and creasing of the land, scorching breezes that pass tauntingly overhead and noisy crickets that make you imagine that you may never drink cool water again. I entered, climbed the stairs and turned to my left. I simply felt her presence. We were alone but the fresh flowers and candles burning round her feet implied that this one-to-one salvation wasn't going to last for an eternity.

'Señora,' I commenced, 'I am content. I come because I wished to light a candle and I was curious to see you, the Patroness, for myself.'

She looked at me intensely as if working some magic upon me. She wore a cape of copper and gold that glinted softly. It draped beyond her feet and over her crown plinth. The infant Jesus was cradled in her left arm. In her right hand she held forward a cross. A richly embellished crown capped this charitable lady. The glass case in which she was kept was placed between two polished-marble columns. Rays of light penetrated through the high church windows onto this humble chapel. Somehow, her

golden colours came to life against a turquoise background. I sat for some time in complete silence.

We were interrupted by footsteps below, echoing round the church. I looked up at the Virgin for the last time. A freak wind caught one of the candles, it flickered and I thought I saw a purple light round her head. I placed some happy sunflowers next to her and thanked her for her time.

Once outside, I was back in brilliant sunlight and squinting. I sat on the church steps, lost in thought. England is a faithless society. Scepticism surrounding religion is immense – except among many of the older generations. Is it a bad thing to be a believer or to seek some comfort in the obscurity of the unknown? In Europe, we possess all we truly desire, in the material sense. We also have relative security; internal threats, or from the outside World, just seem too improbable. Maybe all these comforts have reduced our need to believe and share a faith, even a family nucleus? Certainly, by the men and women in the dustier and dirtier places of this World, scraping for basic human rights and fighting for dreams of land and freedom, prayers are whispered with unfaltering passion. Someone/something/somewhere is believed to be listening.

I remembered as a boy getting trapped on Snowdon with my mother and sister when a thick mist suddenly confronted us on the summit. Visibility was too poor to move down from the mountaintop. Our predicament lasted for an eternity, or so it seemed, during which time I reached a mental state of fear and exhaustion. I remember crossing my hands in front of me and whispering a prayer to whatever god chose to console me. I asked for Hope. That glimmer, that break in the sky.

Surely this is what it's all about - Hope, Esperanza. Shortly thereafter, the mist cleared sufficiently for us to get down to the lower slopes and to a mountain pub with an open fire and Irish coffee. I now know that it was the Virgin of Charity in Cuba

who reached out to guide us. I am a believer; in what I'm not sure. But I know that I'm not a faithless person. I've travelled amid too many cultures, seen first hand so many people who have to believe in order to survive. I've seen guerrilla fighters in Ayacucho, Peru go to church with machine guns strapped round their shoulders. This may be shocking in a place of harmony and worship, but for many people the struggle through life demands faith.

The Virgin of Charity became Cuba's icon of faith for all walks of Cuban society, including the Afro-Cuban religion. From out of a beautifully tragic story she was born, at a time when faith was what most people needed, as it still is in contemporary Cuba.

Rebel Radio – Sierra Maestra

I approached the Sierra Maestra from the town of Bayamo. Every Cuban town has a hero. In Bayamo it's Carlos Manuel de Céspedes, who revolted against Spanish rule and slavery in the 'first war of independence' in 1868. He freed his slaves and marched into sporadic battles until his untimely death. Today, Bayamo is sleepy and peaceful. It is rumoured to sow the seeds from which flower Cuba's most beautiful mulattas.

From Bayamo, I entered the Sierra through a town called Bartolomé Masó. I continued upwards to a village called Santo Domingo, travelling in open-backed lorries. It soon became obvious that I was pursuing an isolated road with little mechanical traffic. I spotted donkeys slurping from a pool of water. The vegetation was overbearing. Everything was giant-sized, beautifully coloured and extremely healthy-looking – the palm trees, the blades of grass, the insects...

I was now at the co-ordinates where Castro managed to escape the slaughter, after a Batista air and ground attack that massacred approximately 70 of his initial column, leaving only 12 survivors. Many at this point would have surrendered and given up the ghost. I wondered whether Castro himself hadn't conjured up a brief prayer asking for Hope.

At Santo Domingo I made inquiries about climbing Cuba's highest point, Pico Turquino (2000 m). A young man went off on his Flying Pigeon to make inquiries. He came back with news that this was 'impossible'. I needed official papers as well as an official guide. Furthermore, there was an enfermedad de café. This meant that the entire area was out of bounds except to the military. I never did find out what a 'coffee contamination' was. Bizarre.

The afternoon was drawing to a close, leaving me without any prospects of going anywhere else that day from this coffee-contaminated village. I decided to pursue my quest. I gave the village watchdogs the impression that I was happy about being refused access and walked off in the general direction from which I'd arrived. Once out of sight, I doubled back and followed the river upstream until I arrived at a small village. A little girl was the first person to spot me. She was sitting in a big stone washing basin cooling off as water trickled onto her body. Her mother soon appeared and offered me a chair in the shade while she prepared coffee. I asked her about the coffee contamination. She confirmed that rumours had come her way, but these 'strange' illnesses were announced with regularity. She raised her eyebrow and dropped her voice before whispering, 'This is a military zone, ¿usted entiende?'

Her sentence of secrecy seemed to explain a lot. Everything in Cuba is limited and controlled – even the mountains aren't free to the gaze of the sun and the moon, or open to the step of the wanderer. I rocked on the chair, drinking neat coffee and staring up at the sierra.

'A pity,' I thought. Next her husband appeared from the backyard. We spoke about climbing Pico Turquino. He told me that recently another villager had done it in one day leaving at 5 am and returning at 8 pm. He asked if the controls in Santo Domingo knew I was here. I told him how I'd arrived and left the town. He stared at me with an air of concern, nonetheless, he agreed to take me. We would be back by tomorrow afternoon, if anyone needed to know.

We set off within the half-hour. I took a small rucksack with water, purifying pills, a mag light, a Swiss Army penknife, a cotton sheet that had been made into a light sleeping bag, a T-shirt, jumper and tracksuit bottoms. It rained savagely for approximately half an hour both that afternoon and the following morning. Heavy drops like lead shots broke through the tree foliage and rapped my crown and face. This friendly fire was most welcome in the excessive humid heat. We didn't really sleep, more relaxed and submerged ourselves in the tropical tranquillity.

Pico Turquino is tough going, but not demanding like my previous experiences in the Andes, where my guide and I reached heights of up to 6000 m. The recent trek down to the enchanting waterfall I found more appealing. I guess we both shared a certain uneasiness which marred the trip; knowing that we were illegally wandering in a 'contaminated' zone. Consequently, I pretended to be keen to get up, pause for breath on the summit, grasp a lasting impression and then head back.

On the summit was a bust of José Martí – an awesome place to commemorate Cuba's most celebrated leader of independence. Ironically, very few Cubans, for the time being, will have the opportunity to contemplate the magic of the highest point of their Island. José Martí must be entrusted to protect their independence as he looks on in his poet's pose of solemnity and longevity.

Was that Jamaica I espied sunk low in the haze?

7th May

Again an open-backed peso-paying lorry carried me along the three-hour journey between Bayamo and Holguín. The journey had the same comfort factor as riding on an Indian desert camel, explaining the cheap fare of five Cuban pesos; practically nothing for people possessing Western currency. Being able to speak Spanish and make the Cubans smile is an advantage. The Cuban people emanate a level of humanity that is unique. I have never known such intimacy between people. Consequently, a little flattery will clear you a space as the people shuffle closer together, suffering yet further from the gruelling heat of the rapidly rising sun.

To join the ride, you have to climb a metal ladder welded onto the back railings. Before climbing up, you are a metre and a half below the seating level. This gave me a comical view of everyone's shoes, inching forward like an impoverished miniature army. I loved to study the different footwear: sandals, trainers, military boots, shoes, cowboy boots, high heels, cloth plimsolls and bare feet. The quality varied from polished leather to tatty threads to field stained soles. Of course, I had yet to put faces to the shoe owners. I would often joke to myself when I saw a pair of daintily polished women's shoes next to bare feet. I imagined a señora's discomfort when obliged to get ridiculously close to the rag-and-bone man. To some owners I'd wanted to point out that the soles of their shoes had somehow become detached and no longer supported their uppers. Once on, I would smile and then announce, 'Well, that's me, just my rucksack to follow!'

I would lay it on its back along the floor and suddenly an old señora had a padded seat. For her the service was now first-class.

Once the journey was under way, conversations would be struck up. Someone would be telling a joke or a raconteur would have seized the moment as he/she told a story. While the kilometres were engulfed, you shook with the sporadic movements of the overdriven suspension. Your body learned to absorb the imperfections of the road surface. The suspension on cars from Developing Countries creates a sound and experience that you will never forget.

Communicating with Cubans in the Spanish tongue is essential; it allows you to take part in all that is going on. And it is far more economic, as you can obtain things off the street, rather than having to resort to dollar bars, restaurants, expensive modes of travel, etc. An example of this need was near Holguín's Central Plaza, where I met an English lad who'd said that he was hungry. I bought him one of those atrociously bad peso pizzas from a street seller who had a limited number for sale in a shoulder bag.

'Ah,' the English lad exclaimed in disbelief, 'I've walked past him several times. He made gestures at me but I couldn't fathom him out. I thought he was hassling for cashola. Mmm, great pizza, man.'

Not only was he misunderstanding people, but he was also missing out on the quirky conversations that the Cubans so loved. Jules had felt a 'lemon' in bars. He had resigned himself to learning Spanish when he returned, but on this occasion, language barriers had defeated him. At the end of one particular day when we had found the watering hole, Jules said in a frustrated manner, 'I know this is ignorant, man, but why the bloody hell can't they speak English!'

He beat his cocktail stick against the glass of his favourite rum concoction, a Mojito, and laughed, knowing that he was being outrageous. It was true though – hardly anyone did speak English. This isn't to say that the English are without their fame in Cuba. They are notoriously famous in Cuba for a certain roguish pirate by the name of Henry Morgan. He audaciously patrolled the Island's coastline with his skull-and-crossbones flapping in the wind, always on the lookout for returning Spanish galleons.

In his day, Henry Morgan had a formidable reputation throughout these waters. His fearlessness clearly matched his skill at deception, boarding foreign vessels and making off with oodles of priceless boodle. I have heard it said that he might also have been involved in the transportation of slaves.

Caribbean writer Jean Rhys, who was born in Dominica, wrote the following in her short story 'Mixing Cocktails':

Morgan buried his treasure in the Dominican mountains... A wild place, Dominica. Savage and lost. Just the place for Morgan to hide his treasure in.

So if nobody could catch Morgan or find his buried income, the only action to take was to protect it at source. The Spaniards hastily built fortifications to try to keep the English buccaneer and his crew out. He was eventually captured and hanged in Kingston, and the Jamaicans named a brand of rum after him. When I return home, I must dig out his life history. I wonder if there is a Spanish treasure chest buried in his English garden?

Many Cubans mention 'Los Beatles, Liverpool'. The pronunciation of the word Beatles is so thickly Spanish-accented that it takes several clues before you twig on. Young Cuban bands play Latin covers of Beatles hits in bars. 'Don't Let Me Down' was a song that I often heard. It was interpreted very well, in many different places. Recent years have seen a trend in the remixing of once-popular hits. I bet these Latinized Beatles covers, if recorded in Egrem Studios, Havana could be big sellers.

From the station in Holguín I walked to the central plaza. I sat down and someone passed me a four-sheet newspaper entitled La Luz. Below the title read a caption 'The Special

Supplement of the Bearded Crocodile', and below that 'The May Festival of Holguín, 1998'. This explained why Holguín was so active; people were circulating at a faster pace than in the other Cuban cities. I noticed that the streets were free of cars and a small-sized crew was assembling a stage. An impressively dressed man stopped to talk to me. His said his name was 'Chicatín'. Steady on son, rewind! He spun it by me again 'Chicatín'. He accentuated the syllables in his name over and over with the rhythm of a funky cowbell – 'Chi-ca-tín, Chi-ca-tín, C-hi-ca-tín.' He chuckled loudly.

He had an air about him of a classic jazz dancer or singer. His trousers and waistcoat were brown with white pinstripes; his shirt was like a billowing linen blouse, baggy and off-white. His hair was cropped down to a mahogany-coloured cranium. His most striking feature was his eyes; they were clear blue and contrasted wonderfully with his skin colour, adding greatly to his charm. He told me that he was the resident house singer in the Casa de la Trova, and that his friend, the festival organizer, had a room for ten dollars a night.

'Vamos,' I said. He took me there and there I stayed.

I met Chicatín later on during my stay in Holguín at the Casa de la Trova. When I entered, he was singing to a full house; this was fiesta week after all. In true Cuban style, he announced that his next song was going out to a 'special friend'. That special friend was me. He was quick to label me his special friend, but this ease of contact isn't always a way to your wallet. Chicatín wanted nothing from me other than comradeship. He sang for a living and this song was for his 'amigo-in-passing' to take with him as a souvenir.

In Holguín, the people get from A to B in old-fashioned 'coches', which aren't cars but elegant horse carts. It's a glorious ride along the streets, bidding good afternoon to everyone you pass. I noticed that the women of Holguín went to great trouble to avoid the sun by carrying umbrellas. I'd seen this custom in films, set in the American Wild West. Holguín had a different feel from the rest of Cuba's colonial cities; it emanated an optimism and a grandioso vitality.

Horse carriages continued to ferry the people to the central plaza. The children would scarper off while the gentlemen helped the women down. The colonial façades of the surrounding buildings had huge wooden doors that appeared to unfold, opening like thick book covers into tales of this fabulous city.

Through one set of doors I discovered a famous band called Los Guayaberos, named after the classic Cuban linen shirt. Their lead singer is yet another maestro of the vintage 1950s jazz era. For his 70 or 80 years, he was impeccably dressed, singing his heart out and tapping his Latin rhythms in a pair of bright green Doctor Marten's boots. Behind him was a younger backing singer who delivered the chorus. I was poured some home-distilled rum, more of that backyard stuff that fired you up into an unfocused frenzy.

I pictured the maestro raising a glass to his lips. Suddenly, the frame freezes and you are looking at a wonderful label photo for a commercial bottle of rum. Cuba is the footage and soundtrack to a classic film.

I ventured through another open doorway and discovered a photographic and art exhibition. The door staff were dozing. All was silent. Strange considering the raucousness of the adjacent building. Had the old boy singing with his band in his suit and bright green Doc Marten's really been there? It had not been a figment of my imagination, had it?

I was about to leave when one of the door staff motioned me in. I entered a large room where paintings were hanging with sheets of newspapers draped over them, masking out the work. I lifted each sheet in turn. This momentary unveiling amplified the suspense. As I peeled back one sheet I gradually revealed a portrait of Christ quite blatantly styled on Che. The whites of his eyes were intense like the ugly moment when prey has been isolated and foresees his own death. The backdrop was blood-red. I lifted the sheet yet further and saw an AK47 machine gun strapped to his shoulder, in the place of a cross. This room was weird.

On display in the hallway were black-and-white photos. This time I noticed a photo of Che staring at, through and beyond me. It was the famous still shot of him, in which his contempt for superpower imperialism and World poverty amazingly seem to have been captured within this single frame. The stare of the fighter reaches into you, as do the conviction and passion, the intellect, and moreover the will of a single rebel with a cause – from the Rebel to You. The photo also gave away something that I'd never seen before. The original contains a side profile of a second man wearing shades and the leaves of a palm tree dangle from above the two.

These black-and-white prints were among some of the best photos I'd ever seen on display. Inevitably, they were all taken in Cuba, as very few Cubans ever have the opportunity of travelling outside the land of the 'bearded crocodile'.

The next outing was to yet another oddity in this eccentric city, La Fábrica de Órganos, which is reachable by carriage towards the outskirts of town. This organ factory is a family enterprise belonging to the Cuayo family. Their Spanish ancestors perfected the art of building wooden air organs. They have been producing these organs in Holguín since 1886. Not a lot has changed for over 100 years. The tradition has been passed down to Francisco, Julio, Angel and Eugenio Cuayo, who are responsible for constructing six grand organs and twelve smaller models per year. Both models sell for \$18,000 each. Their workforce totals 24.

The organs are a fair size and can be pushed around on

wheels. The wood is a light cedar and polishes up like a lacquered rooftop in Tuscany. Francisco showed me round the factory with pride, knowing that it is the only musical factory of its kind throughout Cuba.

The organs are very loud and hugely comical. They are also very European in character. Listening to them conjured up thoughts of afternoons spent strolling along the cobbled canal banks of Amsterdam, where one might be tempted to take a seat and gaze at the tulip gardens either side. One would also envisage company, such as a gentleman dipping his newspaper, exposing a mammoth-sized walrus moustache and bidding you a 'Good morning, sir'.

'So do the organs sell to order?' I asked.

Francisco did that familiar sweep of the wrist the Cubans do. This meant he sold them without any problems.

'People are waiting for our organs. But we have set our pace. What we don't have time to finish, our children will finish for us. Our last sale was to a collector in Holland, Amsterdam, I seem to remember.'

'Is it only foreigners who buy them?'

'Oh no, we sell to other provinces throughout Cuba as well. The Casa de la Trova buys them, as well as other cultural houses and state establishments. This one is destined for Paris. I can see it now in Le Moulin Rouge being operated by a peevish Frenchman.'

Manufacturing air-operated organs for eccentrics to collect wasn't all the Cuayo family did. They also tinkered in musical repairs for all kinds of instruments, and they made double basses and Spanish guitars. We entered another workshop and along the facing wall was a row of double basses. I felt as if I was being introduced to the entire Cachao family, all lined up, smiling and self-contented, knowing that they were all maestros of this instrument.

A hole in the roof allowed a channel of sunlight to fall onto them. Dust particles from wood shavings floated in the rays. The sun is the essential ingredient in this deep warm sound. When the strings vibrate on the neck and body and are heard through a PA system, you believe that your kneecaps are rattling down to your ankles. The double bass belongs in the hands of Cuban musicians, as much as the conga drums do.

As I bid my farewells to the Cuayo family, an organ piped up closely followed by a Latin rhythm section. A band had started to jam along with the organ and its operator.

'The Cubans add a piquante Latin spice to everything,' I thought, 'even a wooden air organ!' I flagged down a horse carriage while the organ operator was going at it like a steam locomotive, a conga player was sitting comfortably tapping away, a timbale player added the fills, and a cowbell percussionist banged the beat square on the bar. No guiro!

Holguín is a delightful city, full of such oddities.

Playboy, his Lackey and the Chevrolet Verde y Blanco

'Baja,' instructed the horseman as the carriage came to a halt. I was now at the beginning of a new adventure, a new route that would hopefully lead me out of the creasing heat of the city to the solitude of a beach. I'd now been in Cuba for nearly five weeks and had only once been to a beach. I'd swum in the sea plenty in Havana, jumping from the Malecón. However, I was yet to climb a palm tree, cut down a coconut, crack it open and tip the milk into my mouth or wander across postcard sands and slip into mirror-mosaic waters.

This idyllic setting was, according to my map, about 70 kilometres away. With my heavy rucksack, I set off walking in the hope of catching a lift. After 200 metres, a classic Chevrolet, the Verde y Blanco, pulled up. The driver was middle-aged and his companion was in his mid-20s.

'Where you going?' the young lad asked.

'To a beach,' I replied vaguely, not believing that I had a chance of cadging a 70-kilometre lift.

'Ten dollars, vamos,' said the man.

'Which beach are you heading for?' I said in disbelief.

'Playa Blanca, 25 kilometres from Guardalavaca, but without the nonsense of that place. Tranquil, good moments and good, good food brought to you on the little white beach. Trust me. Lobster cooked on fire. Rico, rico, rico,' explained the man.

He brought his fingertips together and kissed them just as Italians do on cooking adverts.

'OK, I'm with you.' I jumped in and spread myself out across the plush back interior of this classic car. 'This is the life', I thought. I waited for the gears to engage, but we didn't move. Both of them turned inwards and looked at me.

'Something I've done?' I inquired.

'Ten dollars,' replied the man. He had a strong foreign accent when he spoke in Spanish. The background music was romantic - Italian ballads sung to a guitar accompaniment.

'You're Italian?'

'Si, muy bien. Ahora, me paga.'

He looked comical, like a chubby Italian rogue. I figured that I'd string him along a bit.

'I'll pay you five dollars now and five when we arrive.' I entered into the bargain and was enjoying his astonished look. 'You know how business is done in Europe,' I said. 'I'll pay you half now and the rest when we arrive.'

'No, no, no, amigo. This cannot be. You are in Cuba now. We see ten dollars, or no lift.'

I handed the ten-dollar bill over to the Godfather - Padrino, but the lad scooped up the note and the Chevrolet began to chug through the gears. This was fab. I had at least 70 kilometres to enjoy in the famous green-and -white Chevrolet.

The warm breeze swept over me. The road filled the windscreen and the Italian ballads went through the verses. I soon started to assess my two new companions. They obviously worked as a team and knew each other well – comfortable in each other's silences.

'What are your names?' I asked.

'Eduardo,' said the lad. 'He's my compañero, Dino.'

'Ah, delighted to meet you both and thanks for stopping,' I said.

The pair grunted amicably and stared on. Dino wore a baseball cap with the words 'The Revolutionary Spirit' across the back. On the windscreen there was a picture of the Virgin of Charity travelling in a Chevrolet that was blurred to give the effect of high speed. A fluffy crown dangled from the mirror. Eduardo had a face that was typically Cuban. He was light-skinned with hazel eyes, short hazel hair and a trimmed moustache. We began to get acquainted. I could spot Dino checking me out from time to time in the mirror.

'So Dino, are you on holiday?'

'I live here - in Cuba - Santiago, then Mexico and often in Italia. This is Eduardo's car. He runs it for me when I'm about town. You'll see what nice beach, really nice, how peaceful. Then we ask friend to bring us lobster. He knows me from many years back. He only cooks us the best. Rico, muy rico.' He smiled into the mirror and indirectly at me.

I replied, 'I could do with a good meal. I go hungry every day. I have lost my appetite for beans, ham, rice, eggs and pizzas. My trousers are sagging pitifully.'

I remembered a señor I'd met in Centro Havana. He was angrily tapping an old-style booklet against his other hand,

'Thirty-seven years with this ration book. My quotas aren't always available, like today. The shopkeeper over there tells me that no milk has arrived, or eggs. There is plenty of rice and beans though. Bloody rice and beans! ¡Mierda, Mierda - nada má!'

I took him over to a window where a plywood sign indicated that ice creams were on sale. The window had a board displaying the flavours available. The board was like the ones used on word quiz shows, which work by timber slats that slide into recessed grooves. These slats display the many that are currently available. It was common to see a board with spaces for up to 20 different slats, of which only two or three would be occupied, and this wasn't always the truth either. We looked at the board and decided on chocolate ice cream, as advertised by such a slat - 'Chocolate'.

'Two chocolate ice creams, please,' I asked.

'Sorry, only strawberry left.'

'Señora, you have forgotten to remove the slat with chocolate written on it.'

She shrugged. After all, it was a hot afternoon. For two pesos one can't complain, but the señor walked off mumbling to himself and waving his ration book in the air.

Dino looked at me, concern bouncing off the mirror.

'You don't eat well? We eat like kings every day. Today we eat lobster picked out of the sea and eaten within the hour. One hour! Amigo, you will see. Men bring us refreshments too. You like beer? For me, no, beer aggravates my stomach. But men bring beer if you want.'

'Great, I look forward to this feast on the beach.'

'Under the palm trees, in the gentle shade. The sun gives me strong head problems. I have lost hair, you see.'

He lifted up his cap and I could see that he only had hair on the sides of his head. He certainly had a comical air about him, resembling the late Benny Hill.

'Dino is always coming to Cuba,' piped up Eduardo.

'He knows the ins and outs. 1 don't work now, but 1 drive my car and get paid. 1 have family in Miami. They sent me the money to buy this car. 1 love it. Without my car, 1 have nothing.'

'Is it common for Cubans to receive money from family abroad?' 1 asked.

'About twenty per cent of Cubans get money sent from their families, many of whom live in the USA.'

1 sat back in the plush single long seat. This explained a great deal. I'd often wondered how younger Cubans, who do not have the income that we do, always managed to look so cool. A state wage cannot buy cool clothes, watches and shades and support a household at the same time. 1 knew that income from drug racketeering was unlikely, despite what the Western press claim, as Cuba hasn't got a reckless narcotics underworld, if any. The Island is virtually drug-free in comparison with other countries. Obviously, there is contraband trafficking going on, but not everyone can make ends meet by selling false Cohiba cigars, peddling a bici-taxi or cajoling tourists. Practically a fifth of Cuba's population, therefore, receives money from abroad. It all made sense. 1 couldn't believe 1 hadn't figured this out sooner. Eduardo interrupted my thoughts,

'This Chevrolet was made in 1956. It cost me four thousand dollars, slightly more expensive because it has all original parts, and they are all in good working order. How do you think 1 could buy one of these if 1 worked for the State? Now, 1 have the car it makes me money. 1 put by an amount to pay for oil, services, tyres and mechanics while the rest goes on necessities for my family and myself.'

The Chevrolet certainly seemed very sturdy, as if built to last Eduardo's lifetime. 1 also own a 1964 Saint's P1800S classic. Reliable is the verdict. It purred away without a single splutter. My mind was revolving like a machine, typing out telegrams between Cuba and the USA. It must be extremely upsetting to pack your bags, close the door to your house and leave members of your family and your country behind.

Eduardo's uncle was among the 125,000 Cubans who left the Island on the Mariel boatlifts during a five-month period in 1980. Those five months must have given rise to countless disturbing emotional scenes. It must also have been a period of lighted fuses, as both sides launched propaganda wars in the face of the heightened media interest.

Eduardo told me that his uncle was greeted with open arms by US Immigration. He was provided with accommodation, dollars in his pocket, a job and the chance to make of it what he could. He must be happy then?

'Truly,' Eduardo said, as if recalling a letter sent to him, 'no. Sure he has money, he works, but he is living a half-life. His thoughts and memories are still here in Cuba with his family. He is like a lonely character walking a foreign beach. His feet sink into the sand but every time he looks behind him he sees a wave dissolve his footprints. Cubans like to be in their casa. For this, he is nostalgic.'

I guessed the US propaganda must have been powerful. The newly arrived Cubans were well catered for in the hope that they would write home with accounts of how affluent and trouble-free life was on the other side of the Straits of Florida. This kind of letter would have read badly to those who had stayed and supported the Revolution. This process of displacement formed a part of the war that Cubans on both sides have had to endure. It is a war that no longer involves military exchanges, but nonetheless, dirty tactics are in operation, designed to drain the people's morale by tapping away at the human shell until it cracks.

I was now beginning to understand some of the reasons for controlling movement within Cuba. For example, how you must present a national security card when purchasing a train or bus ticket; how the custom officers at the airport had logged the equipment I'd brought over and   detained it until 'further authorization' was given. Although I found this infringement on personal liberty enraging, I was now able to comprehend it. Cuba is fighting an economic war, a philosophical war, an emotional war and a political war against the World's most powerful nation, which, in terms of global distances, is on its doorstep.

As a result, much paranoia and double-checking is prevalent. The government does not want any more sophisticated bombs infiltrating from the USA with the destination of hotel cellars. One such explosion could quickly render the runways of José Martí International Airport barren, killing one of Cuba's most important sources of income, tourism. Alternatively, computers sent in the guise of a donation from friendly nations but riddled with viruses could ruin a company's system. The State has had to take up this position of careful scrutiny. It is offensive because most people mean well, but there is always room for suspicion

The economic war has left Cuba isolated from most of the World. There are signs all over the Island signifying that something dramatic happened during the 1950s and '60s. The Chevrolet Verde y Blanco was perhaps the strongest indicator, in popular material culture, of this isolation. It symbolizes a moment in Cuba's history when the clock that traded time stopped ticking. It was as if Cuba was living a surreal existence; for example, a famous Spanish painter visited the Island in, say, 1562 and fell instantly in love with it. He captured these feelings by painting the backdrop, the essence of his love. Then a North American painter later added to this original work in, say, 1952. The effect of this today is a nation that still travels round living in an array of pastel colours that had dried on the canvas at the moment of application. It was poetry in motion, not the tacky verse of some poetaster, but with words and images sporadically unfolding in intriguing contrasts. Falling in love with Cuba is easily done.

The other telling sign was to be found in bars, where beautiful stainless-steel refrigerators ran the entire length of the back walls. They looked heavy and reliable and opened with a definite click when the handle was pulled upwards. The doors would reflect the faces of the people drinking and the old rotating ceiling fans that cut through the tropical air, like the blades of a Huey helicopter.

A Hatuey beer, named after Cuba's first revolutionary hero, an Indian who led revolts against the settling Spanish, or a daiquiri cocktail cooled your system while your hair was blown back from the front of your face. Once the drinks were downed, you were ready to meet the beat of the street. You stepped forward through time again back into the present.

If the clock that trades in time stopped ticking for Cuba's economy, the time that trades in musical tempo is running double-time. There is no shortage of music. Everyone appears to be inspired by the slightest melody. In the car we fought to be heard over the stereo rather than turning it down. I remembered my little Cuban grandmother Margarita de Castro in Old Havana, who profited from a moment's silence during one of my visits to sing 'Quizas, Quizas, Quizas', ('Perhaps, Perhaps, Perhaps'). I had seen many a double bass being carried through the streets and pianos being wheeled along between concert halls.

When we pulled up at the Playa Blanca beach and the engine was extinguished, I heard the familiar sounds of congas emanating from a hut. Music was even audible from somewhere on a desolate strip of beach. Dino had driven the car onto the sand and parked in the shade of a tree. He jumped out.

'Hey amigo, look around you. Breathe this air. Why, it is bellisima. Don't need to take photos, simply look for long time and remember. Always remember this. OK.'

He laid his towel out in front of the Chevrolet and walked into and disappeared under the sea. We were in a small bay sheltered by headlands on both sides. The breeze sang in the palm trees. The sea was lapping lustfully and tickling away at my trainer-wrinkled toes. The seabed was dotted with darker shades that broke up the turquoise uniformity. It was a postcard setting and the first time since childhood that I had stood on such a lovely beach.

I stripped down to my kecks and ran and dived into the tray of moist pearls. I swam out and turned, treading water while looking back towards the shore. It resembled golden honey on a silver spoon. The waves glistened like keys turning an ancient treasure chest. They were winking at me, telling me to look deeper. So I got the mask, snorkel and speargun.

The underworld was an array of colours, relics of human waste, fish, corals, vegetation, and I spotted a lobster peeping out of a crevice. The speargun was loaded but my heart was filled with compassion. Dino had said that a man he knew was going to prepare us a lobster dish. I was presuming that he had already fished them out of the sea, or bought them at a local market.

The sea was warm and the sun's rays were strong on my back. It was fascinating gliding effortlessly through the water. I have always loved the sea; I was born in front of it and I wish to be buried at sea.

This was very different from the sea of Edward Braithwaite's poem 'Islands' in his aforementioned trilogy, where 'you see/rocks, history's hot/lies, rot/ting hulls, cannon/wheels, the sun's/slums' (The Arrivants, p 204).

My thoughts rambled until I sensed that someone was watching me. I looked towards the beach, where I could just perceive Dino waving his towel to attract my attention. As I approached the others, I could hear Dino talking from under the shade, 'Why you keep me waiting, shouting in the sun like that? I can't stay long time in sun. It makes me drunk, unwell. I don't like. You know our man is bringing to the beach our food. Rich lobster, fried bananas, coconuts with plenty milk, rice, more fish, salad. Here, you want beer? Bring us beer please, only one. I don't like.'

A man I figured to be an onlooker pedalled off on his Flying Pigeon in search of a cool beer. I heard laughter, sweet girl's laughter coming from above the Chevrolet. I looked up and saw two girls in bikinis sitting on a branch of the overhead tree. They obviously found the situation of two foreigners conversing in Spanish together far too humorous to contain themselves for a moment longer. As they climbed down from the tree, I couldn't help but notice from the corner of my eyes two gorgeous bottoms. So it was true what Graham Greene had written in his beloved book Our Man in Havana. I quote:

Cuba turns out beautiful buttocks as if on a conveyor belt.

Elizabeth and María were their names. Frankly, this was turning out to be a splendid afternoon at the beach, full of surprises. For the first time I was forgetting about the decadent charm of Havana's old streets. Suddenly, I realized that it was good to have put that city scene behind me, at least for the time being.

Our food arrived, as Dino had promised, plenty for all. It went down a treat and, before we knew it, a more relaxed sun was upon us. Dino looked knackered from the sun's ferocity but he still had the zest to sit between the girls with his arms round them. This easy and open friendliness that the Cubans radiate is something you soon learn to accept and cherish. I treasured such moments because I knew they were not going to last indefinitely.

The girls were studying at Holguín University with a view to becoming teachers. That evening they had a reunion to get back for. Dino drove us all and announced a forthcoming travel project. The following day we would set off for Baracoa. It would take a full day of travel, but we had no reason to rush. Any beach that beckoned to us en route would be a welcome distraction from the Tarmac. The girls said they would come only as far as Moa, where they'd be staying with their families. Dino protested with full Italian candour, as if his heart had been shattered until I pointed out that at least we all had the whole day together.

The plan was, from Baracoa we would head for a little village called Imías, where Dino had an old friend from several years back - a mariner. After a night there, we would pass by Guantánamo before setting off for the final destination, Santiago de Cuba. I, of course, had already spent a week in this southern metropolis, but I could catch a train there for Havana.

When Dino dropped me at the central plaza, Holguín was on the point of starting the evening's entertainment. A band stepped onto the stage and began performing Cuban Hip-Hop. I was as shocked as the audience appeared to be, but for different reasons. It was reassuring to know that Holguín was blooming with oddities and experimentation. The band was a six-piece that set a funky backing track for the male and female rappers to jump about over-verbally. There was no drum kit, but the congas, bongos, claves, cowbell and double bass provided a heavy sound. After half an hour, when the band left the stage, the applause rose to a peak. Evidently, the public appreciated this new sound. They must have been getting their heads round it, hence they didn't dance – half an hour was insufficient time to absorb this new sound and influence. After all, experimentation and development in Hip-Hop has been going on for at least 20 years in the West.

Next to take centre stage was a Cuban rock band!

Where was Holguín finding these musical youths? The influences were definitely absorbed from the USA, yet the songs had that Latin edge. This melting pot of styles was now commonplace in contemporary US culture. The Cuban and Puerto Rican immigrants in New York are now famous for their Nu Yorica sound, which fuses their traditional Latin song composition with US jazz and heavy black funk grooves.

I remembered walking the streets of Spanish Harlem as a teenager and hearing Nu Yorican Spanish spoken among the dudes hanging out on the streets. A sentence like 'Hey Marcelo, puedes shutear la ventana, man' could be heard from the steps of some doorway. This experience inspired my song 'Mariel Port, Spanish Harlem' (below and to be released on 'Master Sessions 2'). I saw a lot of folk rhymin' riddles, gettin' by hustlin' while on the fiddle and tradin' liqueur for pay in those days.

Harlem was an exciting place, what with the bustling crowds, the racial mix, life on the streets, the ghettoization of mini-Havanas, people chatting the day away, Latin and Hip-Hop music playing from open windows, the smells of foods cooking from both the home and the street stalls. But, as a fleeting visitor, you couldn't relax; you had to remain sharp and informed. It's only when the barrio knows you that you can become more integrated in daily life. I was never there for long enough, unfortunately, as Langston Hughes remains one of my favourite New York poets.

Mariel Port, Spanish Harlem

From an industrial port, passing the Statue of Liberty,
Through the gateway of Freedom, to the Ghetto of the city,
Thousands came, makin' this their domain,
I've seen many brothers from Big-Wigs to Hustlers,
Crossin' these waters, lookin' to see how far it's gonna get us,
Decoratin' these pavements with their hands sunk in pockets.

Mariel port, Mariel port,
To Spanish Harlem.

Brought by the tide, in the mañana they'd rise,
Takin' to the streets, sellin' fruit and Levis,
Bottlin' liqueur, gamblin' an' all amid America's White,
Servin' up cocktails like the Mariel – Harlem Delight.

Mariel port, Mariel port,
To Spanish Harlem.

Now I've done my time, chasin' rumours for a buck,
Duckin' and divin', findin' a whole lot of means to live my ways,
Rhymin' riddles, gettin' by on the fiddle,
No mistakin', thousands came makin' this their domain.

Over on the West Coast and Southern States, the fusion is more Hip-Hop with Mexican culture. The Chicanos often rapped lyrics about being street tuff in White America. Kid Frost was one such artist who set out to express his identity within a mixed Hispanic and US community.

My impression of his art and vibe wasn't that he was disparaging of US society as much as trying to express his role within this segregated pot. It's a pot that is still a long way off melting and achieving cultural fusion. Racial divides are very prominent across the US. This was a far shout from the Cuban rappers in Holguín. Their concerns weren't for racial tolerance or equal social standing, but for justice with particular reference to freedom of speech and movement, World peace and an end to the economic blockade. Such views are both pro and contra Revolutionary Cuba. Cubans, after all, are less concerned with the need to channel passion into defeating racial divides. The blood of a Cuban is African and Spanish-European. (There are no pure Arawak Indians left, as the Spanish butchered most of the indigenous population and the remainder were weakened by European ailments). Yet contemporary Cuba will always evoke smiles and fond memories for me, having seen racial harmony there.

It wasn't always like this, however. Prior to the 1959 Revolution, Cuba was a life for white Rileys, smooth-talkers, gangsters and those visiting Cuba for both legal and illicit holiday entertainment. Late-night casinos made you rich or poor and got you a gorgeous broad if you wanted. Dollars bought you the chance of sophistication in Havana's celebrated nightlife.

This part of history must remain for other books and for future Hollywood films, once relations have been restored. Hollywood directors are no doubt waiting intrepidly for the day to get shooting Che's film and countless others. No shortage of heroes and heroines to be dug out here as source material.

During the concert interval, the sound technician stuck on a cassette of salsa classics. The public roared, reached for partners, twirled, dipped, poised, kissed, shuffled, flowed and banged hips as the back-to-back Latin beats went on into the night - una noche mágica.

The following day on the road, Elizabeth and María left us in Moa. No sooner had the girls left us than Dino pulled up at the side of the road calling out to another girl who took his fancy. This young lady was standing in the middle of the road clutching a clipboard in the hope of getting a lift. Dino whispered into her ear. I saw her nodding, repeating the words 'Vale, vale' (OK, OK) and then she jumped in gaily. We zoomed round to her flat, where she made up a rucksack of clothing and bits and bobs. She was now part of the travel project, or so it appeared. I was confused, but content to be sharing the back seat again.

Baracoa – The Point Of European Discovery, 1492

May 15th 1998 – My Arrival

Baracoa has a cool scene. We coasted into the town under cover of darkness, after a day of beaches, swimming, feasting on coconuts and general whiling away the kilometres in the comfort of the Chevrolet. Circulating the streets of Baracoa, Eduardo stirred from sleep just in the nick of time as the motor suddenly lost its revolutions, spluttered and came to a halt.

'Gasolina,' he explained, jumping out.

Opening the boot, he revealed a stash of bootleg petrol in plastic drums. He got one out and we lifted it up onto its side, resting it on the rear wing. He opened the petrol cap, behind the rear light unit. It was a clever design – to get to the petrol cap you had to pull the hinged rear light down. The tank was behind this hidden point of entry. Eduardo then introduced a plastic tube into the drum and siphoned the petrol out of the drum and into the reserve tank. He then lifted up the bonnet and fiddled with what appeared to be the air filter while Dino turned the engine over. The Chevrolet growled back into life. I noticed how the engine and bodywork were in astonishingly good condition for a 44-year old car. I guess the Caribbean climate must account for so little corrosion.

Baracoa is a smallish place; finding a casa particular - a family-run hostel, wasn't difficult. Personalizing a room had now become second nature to me. The rucksack popped open, followed by my clothing, books, maps, toiletries, alarm clock. It soon looked as if I'd been there for months.

I sensed an ancient colonial air in the streets. The houses were similar to those in Trinidad; in other words, they were of one-and-two floor construction. Many of the streets were cobbled. The striking difference was that the atmosphere was vibrant, bars opened onto the pavements and music could be heard over the patio walls. I entered a patio bar. The evening was still early, yet the bar was becoming like a cosy love nest, with Europeans and Cubans groping each other on the dance floor and round the tables. The band members were young, and rump shakers. The double bass player winked at me to encourage me in on the act. He held his head up, eyes squinting so as to avoid any discomfort from the smoke that was clouding steadily upwards from the big Habano stuffed into the corner of his mouth. It sprung up and down from his lips like a diving board as his fingers pounced over the crafted body of his bass. A lad dancing salsa offered me the hand of his partner.

'My sister,' he said in a high pitched voice.

'Pleased to meet you,' I replied as I took hold of her waist to dance.

She rudely looked away without acknowledging me. I hadn't wished to be put into a situation like this. Suddenly the band stepped up the tempo to 140 beats per minute. She began vibrating from her shoulders right down to her waist and hips, like a sandcastle during a tremor that measured 6.7 on the Richter Scale. I removed my jacket and made an effort to keep up with this racy babe. Fat chance!

When the song ended, I made my way over to the edge of the patio in order to regain my composure. I was sweating. The brother reappeared, resting his hand on my shoulder.

'My sister is looking for somewhere to sleep.'

'What? Are you not from Baracoa then?' I inquired.

'Oh yes.'

'Then why doesn't she go home to yours? Better still, why don't you escort her if there's a problem?'

He smiled at me in disbelief. He realized that I hadn't understood.

'She's outside waiting. Go and speak to her and see for

yourself.'

I was starting to see. Couples everywhere were getting acquainted, including Dino, who was now in full playboy mode with the señorita he'd picked up earlier cadging a lift. He seemed to be ignoring Eduardo, who sat faithfully by his side waiting to inform him that his Mojito was in front of him.

One of the band members mingled and various people stuffed dollar bills inside his guitar body. This distraction gave me the cue I needed to make a sharp exit. Not sharp enough though. As I walked off towards the main plaza, I could hear the brother shouting after me, '¿Qué pasa, amigo? ¿Qué pasa?'

I bought a beer and sat on the bench. There were lots of young people bustling about. I was enjoying this small town that had so much energy and life. I lit up a Punch cigar and observed the Cuban dress code on a Friday night. All ages and both sexes in Cuba dress well. The lads are generally casual and cool. The girls always seem to wear clothes that grip them tightly. The girls with long hair often had it pulled back and secured in a ponytail or tight grip, because of the heat.

Suddenly, my attention was caught by a lad trying to sell me some bits and bobs for a quick buck. I cursed him for interrupting my thoughts and he shrugged, dropped his head and sauntered off into the crowd. Next came Dino's señorita of the night – fille de joie. She had the look of someone who had got herself into a pickle. She sat down politely with her hands crossed over her knees. She wore hot pants and a boob tube.

'Those two are the maximum insult.'

She wanted to say more. I was sure that, whatever the outcome of her story, it was now going to involve me.

'Can I stay in your room tonight? I just can't be with those two.'

Now I too was in a pickle. She saw my absent expression and hesitated before saying, 'He's offered to pay me. He wants me to accompany him to Santiago. Then I'll return home.'

I felt put out. She was obviously in Baracoa as Dino's sexual amusement. My suspicion arose when I thought I'd heard them talking while showering together before going out for the evening. I was considering my position when Dino came and joined us. He immediately started talking to her in an anxious manner. Indeed this was an anxious moment for the jaded playboy. He would need to pull out all the stops if he was going to convince this young lady that there was still plenty of mileage left on the clock of this 50-something-year-old banger. I left them talking and retired.

I must have been asleep for some time when a knock at the door startled me. It was Eduardo in revolting tight blue briefs,

'Come. Come to Dino's room,' he beckoned, grinning.

'Eduardo, I'm in bed trying to sleep, amigo.'

'Come and see. Dino wants you.'

'What is it?'

'Just come and see, OK?'

'OK. I'll be with you in a second.'

'Don't let us down.'

Those were Eduardo's final words as he retreated down the passageway that led to their room.

Half asleep I got up and slipped on some jeans. I was securing my belt when I tapped lightly on their bedroom door and entered. I thought I'd walked in on a film shoot for a small-time pornographic camcorder-style movie. The bedside lamp was providing a sickening yellowish light. My vision was momentarily blurred as my pupils dilated. I focused on the double bed. Dino had his buttocks in the air and was bent over the girl kissing her breasts mischievously. I could make out tufts of black hairs over his back.

Dino turned round, grinning naughtily. He invited me to join in the ménage à trois. I looked at the girl. For a shocking second our eyes met.

'Come,' repeated Dino.

I shook my head. 'This isn't my scene.'

'OK, leave then,' exclaimed Dino.

I failed to sleep much after that.

Dino was certainly looking after his lackey by casting more than an air of authority over him, feeding him and paying his wages. He was also affording him a share of his pleasures.

Passing Entry

This is tough. I no longer wish to remain in the company of these two base individuals. I went to the bus station to inquire about buses to Santiago this morning. The service is very poor and has a two-week reservation list. I'm afraid that I have little choice other than to sit out the remainder of the coastal journey with them, until I can take a train from Santiago. What ever happened to romance – however fleeting? I love cruising in the car though. Between the front and back seats is a distance – a World apart. This won't endure for many more days. I think a lot of sex tourism goes on in Cuba; you see it everywhere and it is very damaging for the country as a whole: History Repeating – pre-Revolution vices are back in force.

Baracoa has a cultural history that needed exploring. This was the place that Christopher Columbus first happened upon; it provided the backdrop for what the crew of the three galleons Columbus captained espied after nearly five weeks at sea. This was the first time Europeans had sailed substantially west, believing that there was an alternative route west to the Indies. The voyage, funded by the Spanish King Ferdinand and Queen Isabella, was well documented by Columbus and other crew members. Their accounts were later published by the mainland

Spanish press. This point of contact with land was the New World that a humble, but ambitious Genovese sailor-come-explorer had promised them he would find.

It was rumoured that Columbus planted a cross here on the beach in 1492 and I wished to discover the truth about its existence. I also wished to see the River of Honey that ran into Baracoa's densely green coastal plane.

Coming out of the house, I could smell the salt on the breeze. It was already hot and the streets were buzzing like a mini-Havana. At the seafront, I was surprised to find a Malecón similar to the one in Havana, but in better condition and more petite. Further along the Malecón and across the bay, I could see a headland of thick greenery with lofty palm trees standing proud like army generals with dreadlocks. The sea lapped against the rocks like a record needle stuck in the locking groove. The hour was perfect for a stroll.

As I approached the town centre, the ruckus made by the crowds of people grew stronger. Although the Malecón was peaceful, it was obvious that, a couple of blocks further up, a lively Saturday scene was developing. I turned up a street and came across hordes of people queuing outside a dollar shop. Gone was the orderly system of queuing that Cubans normally adhere to by shouting out '¿el último?' - who's the last person? - before joining the end. Instead, there was a frenzied havoc. The shop had a doorman who was keeping the crowds out by lock and key. When two people left, two more entered. This was how the Saturday shopping system worked.

Inside the shop people were browsing while the cashiers looked bored. Television sets occupying an entire wall captured the attention of most of the Saturday shoppers. The price tags were around $400 each. Most of these people were clearly window-shoppers. It was bizarre to see people queuing to see material goods on display, and with such enthusiasm.

One block along, I spotted a wooden sign saying 'Casa del Chocolate' hanging above a large corner building. I looked in and saw an open-plan floor space with tables full of all types of people. Behind a wooden counter was a lady balancing a tray in the palm of her hand. She was offloading bars of chocolate into a brick shaped pile ready to place in the refrigerator. This was sufficient to entice me in. I pulled up a chair at a busy table and everyone greeted me. A waitress came over and I excitedly said, 'I'll have the same as everyone on this table, please, and a bar of that chocolate too.'

Within minutes I was drinking chocolate, eating chocolate ice cream and conversing about chocolate among all those around me.

'Mmm.'

'How rich.'

'How sweet.'

'My favourite.'

'I've got chocolate all round my face and on my hands.'

'This place is heaven-inspired!'

'¡Qué rico, verdad!'

The chocolate talk went on until I started inquiring about Columbus. An old man next to me had a knowledgable air. Local history was etched into the lines on his face.

'Señor,' I said, licking chocolate from round my lips, 'have you heard of the River of Honey?'

His mouth was clogged up with chocolate. I looked anxiously at him as he tried to free his mouth by masticating. He signalled with his hand that he had something to tell me.

'Si, si,' he mumbled. 'You'll come across it on the main road out of town. It's not far. There will be many people swimming in it at this end. Walk upstream and pretty soon you'll find it in tranquillity.'

'How about the cross that Christopher Columbus is

rumoured to have placed in the Bay of Baracoa when he disembarked?'

'Ah, you are seeking out La Cruz de la Parra, what a little treasu—.'

'It exists then?' I interrupted excitedly.

'You will find it in the Church de la Asunción in the small Central Park. We're lucky it's still with us because the church was sacked and partly destroyed by pirates in 1652. Their leader was a notorious English pirate.'

I had a sudden suspicion that this pirate might have gone under the name of Henry Morgan. It wasn't the first time that I was hearing about the misdemeanours of the wild bunch he captained.

'The Central Park is a stone's throw from here. You'll see the market that stretches more or less down to the town's extremity. At the end of the Malecón, before the beach starts, is a monument in memory of Christopher Columbus, which might also be of interest to you. The road to the River of Honey is behind the beach.'

The Central Park was a portrait in itself that could have represented the whole of Spanish America. Large trees cast a shadow over a crowded square of many colours. People talked loudly amid the hustle and bustle of the market. The Church de la Asunción had a subdued neglected atmosphere. It failed to dominate the plaza, as they were designed to do, with their grand bell towers and intricate façades evoking the glory of god. Instead it tended to wilt into the background, like a yellow sunflower in need of a drop of water.

The bells hung in the towers forlornly, as if praying that they could swing into existence and sing again. The towers were no longer bright yellow, but a cigarette-stained off-yellow, like the ceiling in my grandmother's front room. Plaster had fallen and exposed patches of small brickwork typical of Arabic-Andalucian

Artemudejár construction. However, it was a perfect little church for this animated setting, dating back to 1512. I tried the door but it wouldn't budge an inch. I guessed my luck had dried up along with my optimism, when I remembered something an Argentinian friend used to say, 'You have to make the best out of pessimistic moments.'

I stood back from the door and saw a huge keyhole. I put my eye to it. In the channelled vision was the modest little altarpiece. To the left I espied a wee wooden cross that appeared to have some special decoration carved into it, as well as some footnotes. This must have been Columbus' cross – La Cruz de la Parra – that he had planted in the Bay upon disembarkation.

It was a beautifully limiting way to have seen the cross. I remained with my eye to the keyhole for several minutes, absorbed by the peace that the church's interior emanated before turning to face the plaza. I imagined that this bustling market scene must have been similar in the days when Baracoa was first being developed.

The road running parallel to the church, to the left, carried on the market activity. At the end of this road was a little park area with benches. The attraction here was a glorious view of Baracoa's unspoilt bay, with its wild headland and sea horizon and the bust of Columbus.

I walked the length of the Bay along the shoreline before being stumped by a river outlet. The only way across was a wooden bridge - a short distance upstream. The left side of the bridge had collapsed and from here it sloped dramatically down into the river's current. I edged my way over and set off to explore the headland with a hope of looking back towards the shoreline and Bay of Baracoa. This might well have been the view that some of Columbus' crew had etched in their memories when they returned to Europe. I also wished to carry the memories of this charming town back to Europe, along with an idea of what the adventurers might have thought when they saw the New World for the first time.

There was a path - a camino - that skirted the rocky headland. The sea came right up to the rock ledges. Every so often there was a break with a sandy little pocket. The vegetation was thick and luscious and filled with life. I had the impression that millions of eyes were spying on me. Songs and shrill cries could be heard. On a coarse spear-shaped leaf I found the most beautiful snail I'd ever seen. Its shell was decorated in the finest, brightest, most eye-catching colours possible – pink, white and blue. In 34 degrees Celsius, it jumped out of the brilliant sunlight, glowing fluorescent.

When I arrived at the tip of the headland, sweat was pouring from under my hair and running down my face and neck. The sweeping panoramic view was breathtaking. I reflected on a chapter Columbus wrote in his diary, entitled 'The First Voyage to America':

> ... and it was, he says, a great pleasure to see
> those green plants and groves and the birds, for
> he could not leave to go back. He says that the
> island is the most beautiful that eyes have ever
> seen: full of good harbours, deep rivers and the
> sea appeared as if it must never rise...

The only considerable difference today must be that Baracoa had grown. It was bigger in a positive way for, as I looked across the bay, I could still see a simple and relaxed town. No ugly tower blocks stood up; just a purple glow of heat haze encapsulated the whole town. Baracoa possesses something special and magical, well deserving of this glowing luminous crown.

I crouched on a rock ledge and drifted into fantasy. This was a goal that I had longed to fulfil, having already been inside

Columbus' tiny town house in Genoa, having been to Sevilla, Andalucía, where Columbus' fleet set sail from, descending the Guadalquivir River to the mouth of the Atlantic. The fleet then passed many uncertain weeks at sea until this very point rose out of the morning mist, overcoming the sailors' powers of sensation. Cuba was the doorway to the New World they had sought and it was more beautiful than ever imagined. I was at the exact point where the history of the Americas was to change indefinitely. The said date was October 27th 1492.

I made a wish and cast a three-peso coin into the sea. The face of Che Guevara glistened as it slowly tick-tacked down and away to the ocean's depths. It was time to find the River of Honey and cool off.

Walking back across the bay was tougher than when I'd initially set off. My footprints sank deeper into the sandy shingle as if something was purposely trying to pull me down. Back on the Malecón, I jumped onto the wall to get the best view, but a car siren playing a Latinized Dukes of Hazard melody sounded from close by. I recognized this instantaneously as Eduardo's Chevrolet - the Verde y Blanco. Dino was out like a flash and approaching me with his hands wide open. He said, 'Hermano, hermano, we drive all morning looking for you. You upset with us? No worry, we make good today. Trust in Dino.'

I sighed and said that I was about to go to the River of Honey. He offered to drive and find us a decent spot upriver. Once at the river, Dino drove right down to the edge so that the front wheels were partially submerged. Eduardo was resigned to the task of cleaning up his 1950s gem.

I was no sooner out of the car than in the water, which was chest-high and clean. I was soon talking to a group of young students, as the current whipped round us. I was introduced to a young woman called Anisleysis who wished to know more about my stay in Havana and the recordings I'd made with the Maestros.

She was from Havana and visiting family for a break. She taught primary schoolchildren in a central district, having moved to the capital two years previously, although her family roots are in Baracoa and Guantánamo. She was tall, with a rounded figure. Her hair was velvety black, long and wavy and her brown eyes had that powerfully attractive Cuban sparkle. They drew you in, hook, line and sinker, like a fisherman's weighted net.

I made her laugh with jokes about the old Maestros in Sonocaribe Studio and my nights out with Havana's street rogues. I told her about my final wish before leaving Cuba: how I wanted to stroll along the Malecón at dusk with a beautiful Cuban girl. She smiled and her teeth shone a brilliant white against her olive skin, morning coffee eyes and black hair. Make no bones about it, Anisleysis was an outstandingly pretty woman who emanated a confidence in her personality.

'I've done what you dream of and it's all a dream should be – mysterious, spontaneous, exciting, uncontrollable and beautiful movements... mmm... you can make of it what you wish,' she said.

I didn't entirely follow her meaning, and so I asked, 'Where do you live in Havana?'

'Centro, with close friends of the family. I have a medium-sized room to myself. I like a little private space that I can call my own. My life is OK, but pay is poor. You're probably aware of the problems we face during the Special Period. Seven years ago life was great.'

'Do you go out much in the evenings?'

'Oh yes. I love disco music. We go to the clubs and bars around the Capitolio and towards the railway station in Old Havana. We Cubans get in free, so it's a great night out.'

'When are you returning?' I inquired.

'Oh, I have a month's free holiday. I'm open to what life brings me.'

Anisleysis was showing the same spontaneity as so many Cubans that I'd come across. Often they would put off what they were doing for another day. In Santiago de Cuba, I bought some old salsa records from a certain Señor José Carrasco. We spent a great half-hour together digging through his collection and spinning the jaded discs. After purchasing them I asked if he'd care to join me for a beer. José quickly shut up shop and in no time we were under the ceiling fan of a bar drinking chilled bottled Hatuey beer. As the afternoon progressed, he went through a bit of his life story and got rapidly drunk before finally standing up and confessing that he never drank beer. When I asked him why he was on this occasion, he replied, 'I am keeping you company because I have plenty to talk about. Now the beer has risen to my head and I best go home to sleep it off.'

Saturday evening in Baracoa was electric. This really is a great place – friendly, loads to do, beautiful sea, vibrant little colonial streets and wonderful countryside and clean rivers. After dining together, Anisleysis and I happened upon the Casa de la Trova. We walked into a jostling crowd and a band that were as drunk as skunks. I took her by the hand and hips and danced carefully in the space we'd managed to create. She swirled me round. My eyes managed to focus on the old black-and-white photos on the walls. They were all of the famous Trovadores that had passed through these doors. The bandleader winked several times at me. I wasn't sure what he was hinting at until a break between songs when he rubbed his forearm with his two fingers and said, 'Te felicito por tu gusto, caballero [I congratulate you on your taste].'

He winked again and started up the next song.

Anisleysis was the lady dressed in orange-red with glossy black hair. Tonight she was a song unto herself.

Next stop was at a rooftop disco in a colonial mansion. The dance music came care of a DJ up on a platform. Rotating lights bounced over the tops of the people's heads like pebbles skimmed across a moonlit lake. There was no caressing and rhythmic hip jiving to salsa here; the music was foot-to-the-floor bass drums and Cuba's youth was relishing it. We bounced along happily like this for a couple of hours until the music stopped and the plugs were pulled. The club was over and, quite literally, within five minutes the rooftop was empty. We walked to the roof's edge and hung over the parapet wall, looking down onto the street. Silence-

The morning was opening up fast.

On the way back to Anisleysis', we came across the winking bandleader strumming ballads to his friends on a porch. I ran back to the pension and grabbed some beers and a coffee liqueur. The Trovador and his amigos played on until the small hours faded away. The revolution was complete, a new day was in the making.

Cuba is the land of miracles.

The following day, Dino rose in a bad mood cursing the owner of the pension, who lived downstairs, because he had requested a double payment from Dino, having cottoned on to Dino's antics. In the heat of the argument, Dino abruptly decided that we were going to move on to Santiago. Santiago was the end of the road for me in the Chevrolet. From then on, I was back on the iron road and free from their company.

Hence, this came as both good and bad news for me, as I had just had the good fortune to meet Anisleysis. We discussed our options, but the fact remained that I had to return to Havana soon to catch my flight home. I said goodbye with a hope that we would meet in Havana within the next four days. I gave her my contact address at Radio Rebelde.

I left with the suspicion that I might never see her again. Her smile remains vividly engraved in my memory.

On the road to Santiago, we passed through Guantánamo. We pulled over alongside the Cuban security entrance gate to the fence that, in turn, enclosed a US security fence, which was the boundary of the US Marine base. I saw a dozen Cuban troops stationed outside the entrance. The US high-security fence loomed lugubriously in the background and was guarded by US troops.

Such a defensive measure was taken to protect the US' splice of Cuban territory that had been signed over to the US government on a long-term lease in 1903. Eduardo informed me that this base on Cuban territory was the worst insult dealt by the US to Cuba. It was a thorn causing a septic sore in the crocodile's side. He also told me that the no-man's-land between the two security fences was the most densely planted land-mine terrain in the World.

The US naval base at Guantánamo has also been the scene to a number of strange events. Cuba's former military dictator, Batista, used the US base with permission to refuel his bombers during their air campaign against Castro and his Revolutionaries. In fact, the attacks were ill-conceived sporadic bombing missions that resulted in the deaths of many villagers. Evidence of civilian targets can be seen in museums throughout Cuba, in particular El Museo de la Revolución, Old Havana.

The US base also supplied Batista's forces with munitions. Taking all this into account, Castro declared the area off limits and stepped up vigilance along the Cuban side of the perimeter fence. Cactuses, with more prickles than sense, were planted the length of the northeastern perimeter in 1961. This became known, not as the Socialists' Iron Curtain, but as the Cactus Curtain, and was intended to hinder Cubans trying to get into the US base.

Eduardo took us round the base perimeter and onto a beach. It wasn't the type of beach I had in mind. It is patrolled night and day by armed Cuban soldiers. Eduardo explained that many bolseros (rafters) had tried to paddle or swim the distance to the inlet of the US base from this beach. Over the decades a great number had been successful. The USA neither acknowledges nor denies the existence of escaping exiles. Many of the Cuban bolseros who eventually made it to the US base later drifted into mainstream US society.

In 1964, the Cuban Government plugged the base's water supply, which had previously been fed by rivers from outside the perimeter. The US failed to find any underground water pockets to tap into and so, from that moment on, they were obliged to import 'everything', in the complete sense of the word, from the US mainland to the base.

The costs of such self-sufficiency must be staggeringly high. The US' objectives in having a military base on Cuban property are stated as follows in the lease:

> to enable the United States to maintain
> the independence of Cuba, and to protect
> the people thereof, as well as for its
> own defence, the Cuban Government will sell
> or lease to the United States the lands
> necessary...

Camagüey and onto Santa Clara

The train departed Santiago four hours late at 7.30 pm. Eduardo and Dino dropped me at the station. As the Chevrolet stood purring, we said our goodbyes. Dino informed me that their original intention had been to rob me during the trip by driving off with my belongings while I was out of the car. They'd certainly had plenty of opportunity to do so, but they had decided that my company was worth keeping until the end of the road.

Dino himself was shortly leaving for business in Mexico. He said that I couldn't have his address. I told him that I didn't want it. He looked upset to hear this. He suddenly advised me that he was in the sugar industry and then he asked my opinion on himself. I told him that what he was doing in Cuba was seedy and displeasing. I asked him if he lived the same debauched lifestyle back in Italy. I told him that he lacked respect for women and that he abused Cuban hospitality and their current tough situation. He looked vacantly at me with his jaw drooping. I walked towards the station gates.

Once on the train, I noticed that there was a large number of army Generals accompanied by their wives in the carriages. Everyone seemed friendly enough. The Generals were impeccably dressed, their uniforms well brushed with shining polished buttons. Their wives were equally presentable – all dresses and jewellery and strong perfume.

The train rattled on with a rhythm of triplets. When a female carriage guard announced Camagüey, I made a fast decision to spend the night there. I arrived into the night and headed straight for the Gran Hotel in Street Maceo.

Nothing bizarre happened to me in Camagüey. What could I expect? I was passing on a puff of locomotive steam. However, Camagüey was the cleanest city I'd come across in Cuba. The streets are colourful and built on an irregular pattern, which made it far more intriguing than the usual Spanish grid pattern. A church always seemed to appear at the end of a street.

Camagüey was also the home to Cuba's national Afro-Cuban poet Nicolás Guillén, who died in 1989. I visited his two houses in the heart of the city and discovered a little more about his life, having studied his poems at university in Spain.

The famous Trovador, Carlos Puebla, was also a regular guest at Camagüey's Casa de la Trova. His photos line the entrance walls. He was famed for his bolshie romantic compositions, which became a musical chronology of the Cuban Revolution. He wrote the song 'Hasta Siempre' in memory of Che Guevara.

I have this album. The cover shows him dressed in combat gear, a beret and boots. He is strumming his guitar and looking back towards past days. He recorded this album in the same studio as our project. The engineer told me that he was asked several times a day while recording to stop spitting on the studio carpet whenever he felt the need, or one of the other musicians made a mistake. The studio crew laughed loudly at this recollection. They called him El Escupidor – the spitter.

Camagüey had a settled air of tranquillity best observed from the top-floor restaurant in the elegant colonial building, El Gran Hotel. The restaurant has a surrounding wooden balcony from which you can look out over the entire city. I wished I could have stayed longer in this very cheap and fanciful city.

Back on the train to Santa Clara. It was two in the morning when I arrived there. My sole purpose was to visit Che Guevara's new mausoleum and then continue straight on to Havana by bus. My visit would be brief. For this reason, I chose to sit out the early-morning hours below the monument erected in memory of Che.

These small hours spent beside my hero's final resting place were a repetition of an experience that I'd had back in 1994, the difference being that in 1994 I'd been in Bolivia trekking through semi-jungle, retracing the last few weeks of his failed continental uprising; what Che called 'Latin America's Socialist Revolution'.

This journey had led me to where Che Guevara was then buried. The adventure culminated by the side of a dirt airstrip in La Higuera, Vallegrande, Southern Bolivia. The place was hellishly pitiful, dusty and extremely poor. It was here that Che's body, along with the other executed guerrillas, had been thrown into an unmarked mass grave. This information was according to a woman I'd met in London, who cannot be named. She gave me a map pinning down the co-ordinates of his body. She advised caution as the World at large was, at that time, still denied the exact location of Che's remains. An intrigue I was too naïve to comprehend then.

One special day I downloaded my e-mail and the following message from a London lawyer appeared:

Che Guevara's Bolivian Diary

From 1984 for 2 years, Che's last campaign was fought: in London. I fought in it. The fight was for ownership of his diaries written during the Bolivian Campaign. The last entry ended shortly before his execution. His fight had been for the poor, his enemies both Communism & Capitalism, his downfall was the lack of interest in either. Yet nearly 20 years later in London, Sotheby's received bomb threats, the press went wild, but like the Bolivian campaign this London Campaign just petered out.

Even so, mention the name 'Che Guevara' today and everyone (save for the few that are hard of hearing or just plain dumb: 'Sheikh who?') still wants to listen.

I touched the diaries; pathetic, ill-assorted notebooks filled with true, scrawling, doctor's handwriting, like all the worldlike jumble you would find in an attic. There was no hint of grandeur or pomp, just scribblings. Yet I will never forget them. There was something so human, so lovable and so sad.

Bolivia has it that they are 'Documents of State', perhaps they are, but they look more fitting for the shoe box in which it is rumoured they lay for many years.

I know they were.

Viva Guevara, may your compassion fill the world.

This lawyer had been partly responsible for the preservation of Che Guevara's 'Bolivian Diary'. It was not a feat without risks; there had been many people/governments who would have liked to see them seized and burned. In the end, the diary notes were sold in secret by his very murderers. Today, Che Guevara's Bolivian Diary has become extensively read and translated into many different languages.

Che was murdered on October 9th 1967 in Bolivia. When I arrived in Vallegrande, his body had already been decomposing for nearly 30 years below the dirt airstrip. Again I'd arrived in the petit matin and was compelled to sit the night out in this secret location.

Four years later, I was in Santa Clara, Cuba, experiencing a similar moment. The myth of Che's remains had since been unveiled and, on the 30th anniversary of his murder, he was finally given a proper burial in the land of his greatly loved and adopted country.

In reference to the Cuban people, Che wrote in his final letter to Fidel:

If my final hour finds me under other skies, my last thought will be of this people...

These were intuitive words that contained a haunting ring to them. Through death, Che acquired international status as a hero of mythical proportions. Castro led the ceremonial proceedings for his deceased Comandante and once friend. To this day Castro believes that he can contact Che's spirit and that Che is still with him.

Che's presence in Cuba is ubiquitous, as if he is always there with the people he so loved and who took him in like a son.

The night in Santa Clara was similar to the one I'd passed in Vallegrande – fresh and still, and the sky was ablaze with stars.

Che's monument in the Plaza de la Revolución towered upwards, almost rupturing the starry backdrop. He was frozen clutching his carbine rifle and wearing his symbolic beret. The elevated plinth that supported this statue had the words of Che's leaving letter that Castro read aloud to the nation on October 3rd 1965. I placed my rucksack against the base, so as to prop my back up, and reflected while catching forty winks.

The buzz of traffic woke me at about eight o' clock. Shortly after that, the museum opened and the first tourist bus parked up. The museum is constructed below the monument. The first room is the final resting place for the remains of most of the guerrillas who took part in the doomed Bolivian campaign. Their faces and names are carved on simple plaques. The next room contains displays of Che's life and a collection of artefacts from the other guerrillas on what was their 'final struggle'.

The two most striking objects are Che's green bomber jacket and his beret. The jacket is immaculate, as if it had left the factory only yesterday. I stared long and hard at it, but no further revelations came to light. These two items that went so far towards defining Che's image now appear to have a separate identity of their own.

The mausoleum is a much-frequented and revered affair that now occupies a major chapter in Cuba's history. In many ways, it is only right that Che's remains are to be found in Cuba. Che believed in Cuba and the Cubans loved him. However, 'El Che' the legend was more pronounced, more tragic, more poetic and ideal when he couldn't be pinpointed. He was then a lost hero who had been felled in some faraway hellish country without the fashions that pomp and circumstance necessitate.

The Return to Havana and Farewell

Last Week of May

After nearly six weeks in Cuba's interior, I was back walking the cool streets of Havana. It felt great to be back. For me, Havana defines the overall essence of Cuba; it fuses all the individual elements that comprise the Island's soul. It is also an immensely friendly city where attractions are always to be found within eyeshot.

Mijail, along with the rest of the Radio Rebelde crew, greeted me like a lost adventurer back to recount his tales. Mijail's first news was that my donations to the radio station had been finally released by customs, and that all the items were in full use by the station. At that moment they were cataloguing the CDs and records for the station's library. The CDs and players were a significant addition to the radio station's musical output.

Mijail and I wandered off into the depths of Havana, reunited amigos catching up on the latest news. His daughter had recently turned 15. This is a day of major importance for girls in

X Aniversario del Guerrillero Heroico

Latin America; it is the definitive point of womanhood. Her next grand occasion would be her wedding day. For many Latinas that day may follow shortly thereafter!

True to his nature, Mijail managed to cock this major day up by eating a duff pizza from a street stall. Two hours after consuming it, his stomach turned and he was forced to retire early, vomiting well into the night. He chuckled away at the memory and then corrected himself by saying, 'Ah, a terrible shame, though, it was.'

We sat on the Malecón looking out towards the horizon. All the reasons why I love Havana came surging up. It's such a laid-back capital. Part of the reason for this is that there is so little traffic. The ambience is charming. If you listen carefully, you can hear the rattle of a Chevrolet riding a pothole, a bicycle bell tinkling, the laughter of children as they play baseball in the streets, sweet Spanish vocal tones, the rumour of the sea, shots fired from the castle's cannon across the port... Surrounding us were people enjoying one another's company relaxing, chatting, some young student couples were getting to know each other better, lovers holding hands and looking out to sea. Kids with fishing lines were trying to catch the big one to take home for dinner.

There is also the unspoilt urbanization of the city. I am not referring to the crumbling barrios, where old rubble often litters the streets, although there is something timeless about watching an old couple sauntering down some street in Central Havana, the evening sun shedding its dying rays of colour and warmth upon them. I am referring to the commercialization that has plagued most Western cities and eaten away their souls and family businesses from the core outwards. These huge commercial centres that have been built on the edges of towns and cities, thus forcing people into cars simply do not exist here. Only a smallish number of Cubans have cars anyway, namely those with families abroad.

It is refreshing not to see multinationals in business here and areas marred by obscene multistorey car-park constructions. I remembered some lines by the New York based Hip-Hop band '3rd Base' in their song 'Portrait of an Artist as a Hood'. They express their disbelief in inner-city commercialization when they rap the lines:

> And what about the hood?
> A parking lot where the
> Latin Quarter stood

I have always loved those lines: frank, in rhyme, no frills attached. It was a palpable expression of anger from the street. Like '3rd Base', Jonathan Glancey echoes some of my thoughts on this inner-city ruination in his aforementioned article for The Guardian Newspaper:

Castro or no Castro (and, whatever you think of the man or his regime, he has looked after his city better than almost any other politician in the world), Havana is a remarkable and special community. The moment it is invaded by developers and whorish architects, the poor will be shipped out of the centre, trashy, energy-gobbling office blocks, banal shopping malls, socially divisive luxury hotels will barge in and Havana will become an ace playground for business dudes and Miami vice merchants with quite a nice Spanish Baroque tourist theme town attached. It might not be such a good idea, then, to bridge over those 90 miles of shark-infested waters.

The cultural capacity of Cubans never ceased to amaze me. Their level of awareness is inspiring. Cubans have a World vision that has been attained through a high level of education. It is a sad fact that, for the time being, many Cubans may never be granted the opportunity to leave their Island and discover this vision. Hopefully, this will become possible, with the coming of inevitable change. It's ironic to think that one of their symbols of Hope – Che Guevara, was first and foremost an adventurer.

Che took time out from his doctorate studies in order to satisfy his quest for travel and romance. I often wondered whether his vision for Cuba hadn't been lost or forgotten somewhere down the road towards victory. Hasta la victoria!

We must take into account that the running of a rebel country is not an easy task. Nonetheless, Cubans always prefer to think optimistically. Even their favourite phrase, No es fácil, sigamos luchando [It's not easy, we carry on fighting], was said with moving conviction.

I once spoke to a retired gentleman who kept himself active by bar work. At the bar I asked him for a paper serviette, I only wanted to wipe the sweat off my temple. When I'd finished, he asked my opinion on the recent trade deal signed by the Canadian Prime Minister with regard to investment in Cuba. He didn't wait for a reply, but continued optimistically, 'This is all good news. We are opening up to foreign investors now. We have established ourselves in our country. We know what we have to offer. We know our limits. The time is right for us now. They're starting to come, and on our conditions of mutual respect. The world is realizing our potential and this doesn't involve the US. They are being left out of the game. There will be nothing left for them to buy, develop and trade.'

I pondered for a while before replying, 'But can a country grow on the World market today without the inclusion of the US?'

'Cuba can and will. We have only eleven million people and so much to offer. We want no sympathy, only equality,' he concluded.

In years to come, his words may well ring true. All countries have had their darker and crueller pasts, have leant on others to empower and enrich themselves. After all, historic time isn't equal across the globe, in terms of development and progress – Europe may repeat it all again if some phenomenon sparks it off, or it may be the other way round. History isn't always fact and logical, something that we study and learn never to repeat. What the Cubans do not have today may be abundant in the years to come. And how far Cuba has come since the 'discovery', being lost and won like capital by the various imperial powers, and an economy that was based on the trading of humans. This alone justifies a love for this country, and its rebellious stance that means something deeper: you want Cuba to succeed, grow, integrate and put such a history to the test, to distance itself from such evil and show that it doesn't have to accept this base example of economy.

The very word 'Capital' for many people is tempered by a shadow of darkness:

Do you know why people like me are shy about being capitalists? Well, it's because we, for as long as we have known you, 'were' capital, like bales of cotton and sacks of sugar, and you were the commanding, cruel capitalists, and the memory of this is so strong, the experience so recent, that we can't quite bring ourselves to embrace this idea that you think so much of.

(Jamaica Kincaid, A Small Place, p 37)

With regard to history being beyond any means of justification, Derek Walcott, in his essay 'The Muse of History', writes:

I accept this archipelago of the Americas. I say to the ancestor who sold me, and to the ancestor who bought me, I have no father, I want no such father, although I can understand you, black ghost, white ghost, when you both whisper 'history,' for if I attempt to forgive you both I am falling into your idea of history which justifies and explains and expiates, and it is not mine to forgive, my memory cannot summon any filial love, since your features are anonymous and erased and I have no wish and no power to pardon.

('The Muse Of History', pp 373 and 374)

These are important issues and go some of the way to offering different insights, rather than applying Eurocentric perspectives on the World.

Old Havana was up to its usual trickery. There were a lot of people finding a means of making dollars - some more genuine than others - like a poet I met, Gregorio Plasencia Herrera, who recited me his poems and then sold me his self-published small book for a dollar. I treasure this book. I called in on my little Cuban grandma, Margarita de Castro. We looked over her balcony and onto the famous Calle Obispo. In the book she found a fitting poem with a flavour to suit the moment, entitled 'Buscando el Amor' [In Search of Love]. She read it aloud:

> I walk through life
> Like a wandering adventurer
> In search of a love
> That must be true;
> Of those that exist
> Must not be for love of money
> But where can this be found friend
> If I wander through life
> Always wanting and
> Penniless.

This was a realistic poem for a chimerical character in Havana today. It didn't have the crazed ring to it that Graham Greene's poem had in his aforementioned novel of the 1960s:

A man, wearing a conventional black dinner jacket among the jungle trees like an English district officer was singing:

> 'Sane men surround
> You, old family friends.
> They say the earth is round-
> My madness offends.
> An orange has pips, they say,
> And an apple has rind.
> I say that night is day
> And I've no axe to grind.

> 'Please don't believe...'

(Our Man in Havana, p 89)

At that moment, a young lady shouted up to us. Margarita recognized her as a family friend and she joined us on the balcony. Margarita winked at me. The young lady worked in the Partagás Cigar Factory as a roller. Perfect, as I intended to stock up on cigars before leaving Havana. My Latin friends back home were expecting this of me as we have a tradition every Friday evening, whereby we smoke Cuban cigars, drink Irish beers and chat liberally. I had broken the tradition by departing. However, I felt certain that I would be pardoned once they saw my rucksack containing boxes of fat genuine smokes. They would be sufficient to keep us in conversation for many Friday evenings to come! I couldn't wait to tell my fellow cigar puffers that I'd met one of the ladies who actually rolls them.

She said she'd be at the factory the following day, so why didn't I come along for a visit. I clarified one point that must vex every visitor to Cuba - is it worth buying cigars from the many touts in the street who offer boxes at greatly reduced prices? She was quick to respond, 'They're all false, although still a fine enough smoke, if you are offered a decent box. There are no guarantees with contraband; quality varies. What happens is that the finished cigars pass through quality control, where they are scrutinized for size, presentation and finish. Only the best ones are packed for exporting, as it is imperative that Habanos live up to their reputation. Those that don't pass often end up as contraband on the streets. At worst, scraps of cut ends are swept from the factory floor and rolled in a complete tidy leaf. Although they look good, these are the worst and smoke like dirty exhaust pipes.'

'But they are presented in sealed boxes as if from a shop, or from export stock. They totally resemble the real McCoy, deceptively so,' I said.

'This is because the boxes, labels, seals of guarantee, cedarwood lining sheets often go astray from the factory premises too. The underground market is a big one here in Cuba, especially for cigars, as their value is high and they are small - they can be moved easily and discreetly. Almost all the contraband cigars for sale on the streets have come from within the factory premises.'

Cigars certainly had an air of intrigue about them, disregarding the myth of where they are rolled, and the stereotypical image of a gangster smoking one in a black pinstriped suit. They are also a status symbol of coolness, collectedness, sophistication and structured rebellion. It wasn't solely the bearded rebels of the '59 Revolution who enhanced their image by smoking a big Roger. I once saw a front-page photo of a US businessman in The Guardian Newspaper, looking side-on at the camera lens with a Habano protruding like a felled tree trunk from his mouth. The caption read:

> You look a mean mother on Wall Street
> with a Habano in your mouth

Of course, Cuban products are illegal in the US and possession of such can secure you a heavy fine or a jail sentence, just as a US citizen who visits Cuba can be fined $250,000. The land of democracy, after all, can tell you where you can and cannot go. The truth is that there are Wah Wah loads of US citizens on the Island. How come they don't get collared when they turn up at US border controls? The answer is that, in this cat-and-mouse game, the Cuban authorities do not stamp US passports, they stamp a piece of official paper instead. This throwaway document is then surrendered on leaving and no one's any the wiser. US citizens pass via Mexico or Canada.

If a cigar with all its packaging can escape factory security and border controls, it is no miracle that a Habano can find its way onto Wall Street. Many of the US Presidents down the line have enjoyed the aroma of a Habano. They probably felt like naughty schoolboys smoking behind the bicycle sheds.

Kennedy's favourite brand was the Petit Upmann and he did look cool with one. Clinton prefers to use his Habanos as a toy, putting them to use as a tickling aid! Remember - Clinton never inhales! Both he and his women like the king-sized Habanos.

Winston Churchill greedily puffed on his quota of seven Habanos a day! This earned him the honour of having an entire brand named after him, enriching the Cuban economy in the process, and emphatically claiming that Habanos were responsible for his sweet agreeable temperament!

Cigars aren't solely a symbol of masculinity - some

women love them too. At Christmas my aunt always smokes a Habano and can't be persuaded to pass it round. She says that it isn't a joint, and fills the room with smoke while letting herself be carried off in reverie. Exactly where her thoughts take her no one knows, but she claims that it's a moment of great composure in her life; she feels cool and sexy. There must be some truth in this, judging by the number of women who said 'yes' when I asked if a cigar made them feel sexy. I think it is the same response for men - a woman smoking a cigar does suggest a level of sophistication and sexiness. Men feel cool and seriously composed. This pastime is certainly more popular with men, but the cigar is wholly dependent for its graceful calibre on the delicate touch of femininity in its creation, its feel and its smoking.

I'd made up my mind to purchase my cigars from the factory shop. I'd smoked enough clandestine ones and, although they are a decent enough smoke, I wished to return to my friends of 'the cigar tradition' and to my aunt with the real McCoys.

The Partagás factory is situated behind the Capitolio building, a landmark of Old Havana styled on the Capitol building in Washington DC. When I arrived in front of the factory, I stood back to admire the colonial façade. The wall was painted in a deep burgundy and a headstone had been chiselled with the company's hallmark. I would have observed more had the cigar touts not spotted me. They came running towards me. One shouted, 'Hey, amigo,' in a cheeky manner, offering me a handshake.

That was it, I was off dashing for the cover of the factory shop, located just inside the main entrance door. They ran after me shouting words to the effect of 'I have real Habanos, good quality. You will come and see. My mother, she works in the factory. We get genuine cigar for you.'

I made it to the factory doors with about eight hopefuls

in hot pursuit. The lady at the security desk shook her head despondently and muttered, half at them, half into her lap, 'Cábrones [Bastards]!'

Inside the shop was a glorious display, exactly as I'd imagined. Almost everything was deep brown: the glass-doored wooden cabinets, the cigars, the poster-label advertisements, the people selling them, the floor and ceiling boards. It had the feel of a classic place where a work of art is presented such as a wine bodega in Spain.

The cigars were mounted in their decorative boxes with their lids open. Behind the till the back wall was stacked to the ceiling with sealed boxes of 25s. I purchased a box of 'Punch' and two boxes of 'Romeo and Julietas'. All the cigars were individually sealed in aluminium tubes so that they wouldn't dry out once back in the UK. I asked the connoisseur serving if I could briefly visit the factory.

'Today, it is not possible as the factory is closed for visits,' she told me.

My experience of Cuba had taught me how to go about things that 'weren't possible'. I exited the shop and went further down the passageway that led into the factory depths. The aroma became sweeter with every advancing step. I approached a well-dressed man as he sat smoking behind a desk immersed in paperwork. We chatted for a while. I explained that I'd been recording music in Cuba and that the following day was my departure date. He capped his pen and led me to the lift, saying, 'Since 1845, this factory has been producing cigars. It was founded by Don Jaime Partagás. Have you bought any, smoked any yet?'

'Yeah. Romeo and Julietas are my favourite brand.'

'Ah, the creation of Señor Pepin, known in his time as "El Romántico". He was an adventurer who gallivanted widely on his horse "Julieta", winning lady's hearts and secret passions. You know that "Cohiba" is said to be the première marque? When Columbus arrived, he found Indians smoking rolled tobacco leaves. They repeated the word "Cohiba" to him and that is how they got their name. Ah, we've arrived at the work floor.'

A plump lady, who sat reading while operating the lift, swung back the safety door for us and we stepped onto an open-plan floor. The area was a hive of activity. Hundreds of rollers sat at desks working their nimble fingers. A magnified grainy voice could be heard over a public-address system. From somewhere, somebody appeared to be reading a novel, or telling a story.

My informal guide continued, 'The workers here are known as fillers and binders. The tobacco leaves arrive here graded and sorted according to size and colour. The filler tobacco is rolled into a bunch like on that desk there. Then a wrapper leaf is trimmed to size and stretched round the filler. The cap, also formed by the wrapper, is stretched round the tip and stuck down. All the wrappers and caps are stuck down by natural glue with a vegetable base.'

I looked along a row of tables as the Torcedores worked their fingers with the rapidity of a flautist running up and down the scales. The tools of the trade come cheap. All I could see on each table was a wooden board, a cutting blade, a tin of glue, a round mould to pack the fillers into and a guillotine for cutting the finished cigars back to precise sizes. The workers were of mixed gender and various age groups. Many of the workers were happily puffing away on the fruits of their labours. At the end of the factory floor was an aged man sitting on a raised platform. He was staring intently through old National-Health-type glasses, reading from a book into a crusty microphone. The workers were listening to him above the low-frequency noise created by the rolling, pasting, cutting and puffing.

'He's reading them a novel to relieve the monotony of the task,' explained my guide. 'Most Torcedores here can roll up to 120 top-quality cigars a day. Sometimes salsa bands come in and play songs that the workers request. We also have cultural and political readings. All this helps to provide a more relaxed work environment. Shall we go up to the next floor and see quality control?'

The quality-control floor layout was compartmentalized into smaller office spaces. Just a bass rumble from deep voices could be heard, and not what was being discussed. It lacked the jovial atmosphere of the workfloor below. The workforce here were responsible for passing or rejecting cigars: a very important position. A rejected cigar means less pesos for the roller, who is paid per cigar. Equally important, a cigar that passes the checks will go for export. It has to be perfect to live up to the reputation that Habanos have internationally.

The inspectors screwed up their eyes and contorted their faces as they checked each one for appearance, weight, colour and diameter. They were then bundled into groups of 50 and given a label attesting to their quality. I wondered at what stage, and by whom, a certain number went missing, to end up on the black market. It was a question that answered itself. Habanos disappear during all the stages of preparation.

I left the Partagás factory as the afternoon drew to a close. Unfortunately, I didn't spot my friend rolling away. Nevertheless, it was a charming way to have whiled away a few hours on my last afternoon in Cuba.

I strolled down Calle Obispo and onto La Plaza de Armas - the epicentre of Old Havana. The market-stall holders were beginning to pack up their bric-a-brac and foxed books into boxes before loading up trolleys and disappearing down the narrow back streets. The screeching of the dry worn-out wheels made the whole laborious routine sound painful. As they disappeared round the corners, I heard a string orchestra practising from in the courtyard of the old palace, now the museum.

I sat on the same protruding stone below the window as I had done on my first afternoon in Havana, when I met those lovable rogues. I listened to the music, the evening sun tickled my face. I laughed at the memory of a great evening spent with people who, between them, had tried to sell me moments, cigars and soap.

The trip had not shattered my faith. My belief, both before and after my trip, is that the trade embargo is wholly cruel, and a crime against humanity. It is an act of uncompromising aggression against a poor tiny neighbouring Island. I read the following article by A. A. Gill in the Sunday Times some time in April 1999 while preparing this manuscript:

The blockade has managed, in a predictably contrary US way, to produce exactly the opposite of its desired effect... The one incontrovertible effect of the US animus has been to keep Castro in power and Cuba locked into a defunct, meaningless, one-sided confrontation.

Perhaps I should make this clear - Cubans are not anti US citizens. They react wholly and purely against US government policy and its hurtful and hindering effects upon them. Why the US government maintains this trade embargo against Cuba in spite of great unease at its existence within the UN is anybody's guess. It seems all the more bizarre when one considers that thousands of US soldiers were killed fighting against Communist Vietnam about the same time that the Cuban-American equation of intrigue came to light and the US now trades with Vietnam.

A country cannot hope to be successful with such overwhelming odds stacked against it: reasons why Castro may never have let alternative power structures co-exist and offer challenges to the ruling order. Therefore, no World leader - US or otherwise - could ever denounce Cuban Socialism and label it as a complete failure, as it was never given a fair chance. Nonetheless, the palpable truths are there, staring at you, and credit must be given where credit is due.

In Cuba, you will not find the desperate poverty that exists in the other Latin American countries. Neither will you find the same degree of foreign dependency and multinational companies operating on the Island - unlike Latin America, which relies so heavily on them.

Finally, and perhaps most significantly, credit should be given to the near, if not total, eradication of racial prejudice within Cuban society. Of this they are justly proud.

Cuba's future: its children continue to grow and benefit from free childcare, education, health care and cultural activities. They are World leaders in the new revolutionary field of biochemistry. Foreign investors are moving in and working with Cuban enterprises; private enterprises are also being allowed to grow. Castro and the city's architects have preserved the architectural wonders for future generations to enjoy, making Havana the oldest capital city in the New World. All this remains in place even during the Special Period. The great level of humanity, culture, colour and sport (Cuba's sporting successes, especially in the field of baseball, are a source of great national pride) attract the World's media time again.

In the meantime, Cubans continue to live optimistically with a 'sense of separateness' which has made them famous, but with an uncertain future. In my view, it won't be a future, as many believe, hailing the return of Cuban-Miami vice. Of course, crime will rise and a degree of humanity will be lost as Cubans move into a more capitalist free-market economy. But other forms of happiness will be generated from greater freedoms. There is one aspect of this Island's soul - the people - that cannot be changed beyond all recognition. Cubans will always sing for hope, they will always fight for sovereignty. Their history has dictated this: Revolution against the master discourses began on October 27th 1492.

I stared out of my bedroom window. Suddenly, I was back sitting on the stone window sill of the old city palace. The mystique and animation of Old Havana came back to life. A young couple cycled past me, the lady sitting cross-legged on the rear pannier frame. I could visualize her sparkling teeth reflecting spectrums of light like an exotic prism. She was creamy in complexion. The man was a mulatto and dressed impeccably in brown and white. He wore a Stetson and kept the lady laughing by rhyming riddles to her. It was like the scene from 'Butch Cassidy and the Sundance Kid' - flirtation two-up on a bicycle. 'Raindrops Keep Falling on My Head' became the soundtrack to the rural scene.

But now I was looking in on a tarnished urban backdrop... some-/thing torn/and new-

...postscript begins... diary source presumed to be rebel not corporate... rebels now thought to be publishing through an organization called 'la prensa rebelde' - 'the rebel press'... stop...next title rumoured to be hot off the press is poetry of 'scenes from an urban wasteland', embracing the themes of displacement, love, race, the street, freedom, revolution and music in eastern europe... stop...also talk of a novel entitled 'the day the prince came'...stop...will keep you informed as to the movements of 'lpr'... stop...message ends...

- 828 7477-